MARCO

ALGARVE

D1778065

with Local Tips

The author's special recommendations are
highlighted in yellow throughout this guide

There are six symbols to help you find your way around this guide:

for Marco Polo recommendations - the best in each category

for all the sites with a great view

for places frequented by the locals

where young people get together

(A1)
map references

follow this route for the best sights in the Algarve

MARCO ⊕ POLO

Other travel guides and language guides in this series:

Amsterdam • Brittany • California • Crete • Cyprus • Florida
Gran Canaria • Mallorca • New York • Paris • Prague
Rhodes • Rome • Tenerife • Turkish Coast

French • German • Italian • Spanish

*Marco Polo would be very interested to hear your
comments and suggestions. Please write to:*

*World Leisure Marketing Ltd
Marco Polo Guides
9 Downing Road, West Meadows
Derby DE21 6HA England*

*Our authors have done their research very carefully, but should any errors or
omissions have occurred, the publisher cannot be held responsible for any injury,
damage or inconvenience suffered due to incorrect information in this guide.*

Cover photograph: Porto de Mós (Mauritius/Susan)
*Photographs: Baumli (39, 43, 46, 49, 72, 86); Hetet (9, 10, 13, 15, 29, 56, 69, 70);
Mauritius: Fischer (22), Kalt (17), Messerschmidt (85), Susan (inside cover, 4, 34, 77, 79),
Thamm (74), Torino (50), Vidler (18, 26, 62); Schapowalow: Heaton (6, 25, 59),
Messerschmidt (37); Thiele (21, 82)*

Cartography: Mairs Geographischer Verlag, Hallwag

1st English edition 1997
© Mairs Geographischer Verlag, Ostfildern Germany
Author: Katja Krabiell
English edition: Cathy Muscat, Emma Kay
Editorial director: Ferdinand Ranft
Design and layout: Thienhaus/Wippermann
Printed in Italy

*All rights reserved. No part of this publication may be reproduced or transmitted in any form or
by any means, electronic or mechanical including photocopying, recording or by any information
storage and retrieval systems without prior permission from the publisher.*

CONTENTS

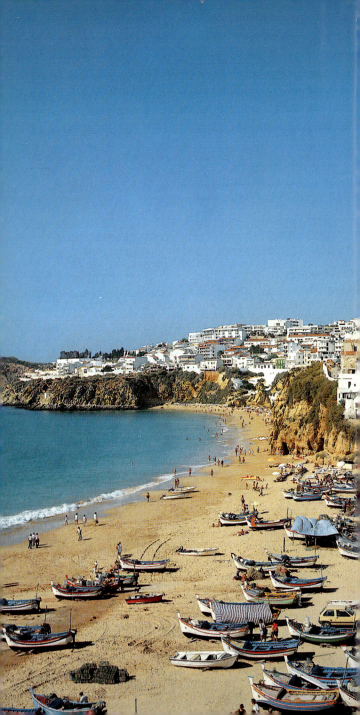

Discover the Algarve

Where the remnants of an Arab civilization blend with the saffron and ochre hues of an exotic landscape

Deep blue skies and crystal clear waters, brightly painted boats and old donkey carts, dreamy coves and almond trees in bloom, sleepy villages and long stretches of golden sand… this is the classic image of the Algarve as presented to us in the enticing holiday brochures. Images of the countless tourist resorts and hotel complexes that have sprung up along the coast and overrun some of the most idyllic corners are, of course, carefully omitted. However, despite the fact that the property developers have succeeded in destroying much of its natural beauty, the 'Portuguese riviera' still has plenty of charm and draws thousands of tourists to its shores each year. Just 15 years ago this area was an uninterrupted paradise. Today, little of the coast has escaped the construction frenzy, but the inland areas remain relatively unspoilt. This is where you will witness the true Portuguese way of life which runs at its own leisurely pace.

Albufeira — the Saint Tropez of Portugal

If it's sun, sea and sand you're after, the Algarve will not disappoint you. Every year, countless sun-worshippers from all over the world flock here during the hot summer months to stake out their own small piece of paradise. Nothing could be more alien to the Portuguese mentality than the frenetic dash for the beach. The Algarvios have a much more easy going attitude and take it all in their stride. In their free time, large groups of family and friends gather together on the less accessible beaches that lie tucked away in the rocky coves. These hidden spots can usually only be reached after a trek along some unmarked path. The atmosphere on these beaches is relaxed and friendly and any visiting stranger who manages to find their way to them are welcomed. The Portuguese are renowned for their hospitality and amiable nature. Despite such an influx of differing cultures, they are very laid back and tolerant of tourists. The only thing about the Portuguese that you might find difficult to get used to is their driving, which is not quite so relaxed!

Daring, courage and faith are among the other national characteristics which, centuries ago, produced some of the world's greatest explorers and navigators and made Portugal into one of the great European colonial powers. In defiance of the commonly held belief that the world ended (*finis terrae*) just south-west of the Iberian Peninsula, the Portuguese sent fully equipped galleons out into the stormy seas in search of new worlds. Passing the rugged cliffs of Cabo de São Vicente, Portugal's most south-westerly point, countless ships sailed into the unending blue of sky and sea.

It was out of this unknown that the Arabs appeared. In 711 AD they invaded and colonized southern Portugal, which they simply referred to as the West – *Al Gharb*. They brought their religion and culture with them and coexisted peacefully with the indigenous population, Christians and Jews alike.

This Moorish migration had a profound effect on the history of Portugal. The influence of the Arabs on this area of land was widespread and lasting, and is still very much in evidence today. Within a few hundred years they had cultivated this wild southern expanse and turned it into a garden of paradise, filled with exotic fruits and sweet smelling flowers. Olive, almond, fig and carob trees were brought over from Africa, along with a variety of other hardy species of plants that could withstand the dry climate. The Arabs dug wells and constructed irrigation systems allowing for the cultivation of mandarins, lemons, oranges and rice (in flooded paddy fields).

Under Arab rule, the Algarve became much more developed than its neighbouring Lusitanian provinces. It benefited from the agricultural skills of the Muslims for five centuries until, in the 13th century, the last Arab em-

Bizarre stacks and grottoes at Ponta de Piedade near Lagos

peror was ousted by King João who declared himself 'King of Portugal and the Algarve', even though they had previously been two separate kingdoms. To this day there still exists a kind of cultural divide between the Algarvios, who speak a cruder form of Portuguese, and the Lisboetas who consider them to be less than refined. Such snobbery, however, doesn't stop the city dwellers from flocking to the Algarve every year, along with the thousands of other holidaymakers from around the world. This is a place where the sun always shines, where the sea is clear and clean (in most places) and washes on to fine sandy beaches, and where, even on the hottest August days, a cool breeze blows.

The Algarve has much to offer every breed of tourist. If it's fun and a good social life you're after, activity and night-life abound in the busy beach resorts. If you have come here in search of peace and tranquillity there are plenty of unspoilt inland havens to be found, and the Californian style reserves will satisfy all nature lovers. Portugal no longer looks to the unexplored Atlantic for the fulfilment of its dreams, and the melancholic words of epic poet Luís de Camões are no longer relevant to this fast-developing country with its solid, tourist based economy. The Algarvios proudly maintain that 'this is where Europe begins'.

The coast of Portugal stretches for some 835 km, and its border with Spain is 1215 km long. The Algarve is the country's smallest province and boasts a unique landscape. Impressive ochre coloured cliffs conceal magical

grottoes carved out by the relentless waves, and hang over fascinating rock formations that rise out of the sea like bizarre sculptures. This enchanting coastal landscape is framed within an impressive mountainous backdrop. The climate is sub-tropical, which means that the summers are long and hot and the winters are characterized by heavy bursts of rain (with lighter warmer rains inland) allowing for a unique variety of plant life to flourish.

The mountain ranges of Monchique and Caldeirão shield the Algarve from the north winds, making the south and east coasts warmer. The swimming conditions here are consequently much better than they are in the west, where the water is rough and unpredictable. Just beyond the coastal strip, running south of the mountains and spreading across the whole province is a limestone ridge known as the *Barrocal*. Most of the land around it is cultivated with crops introduced by the Moors and an abundance of indigenous cork oak trees, as well as walnuts, citrus fruits, and avocados. Pine forests border the beaches, and the river banks are lined with wild oleander. Gardens are overrun with bougainvillaea and the poinsettias are as tall as trees. Streets are lined with plane trees and broom; tamarisks and palms can be seen everywhere, swaying in the evening breeze. The unmistakable scents of oregano, wild mint, rosemary, lavender, and sage fill the air. Spring is hailed with the early flowering of white irises that appear in February, later followed by violet ones. In the middle of spring the fields

HISTORY AT A GLANCE

4000-3000 BC
The Iberians, forefathers of the Berbers, migrate to Portugal. The Lusitanians, a related tribe, settle in the west

1000 BC
The seafaring Phoenicians establish trading posts and settlements, followed by the Greeks and Carthaginians

200 BC–410 AD
Under the rule of Emperor Augustus, the Romans establish a new province with its own laws

5th-6th century AD
Barbarians from central Europe invade the peninsula. One of these groups, the Suevi, establish a kingdom around Braga that reaches as far as Tejo, later destroyed by the Visigoths

711
The Arabs and Berbers (Moors) conquer the Iberian peninsula

9th century
The Christians, who have been forced to withdraw into the north-west, gradually reclaim their land forcing the Moors to retreat. By 850 all of Portugal, apart from the Algarve, is freed

1143
Alfonso Henrique proclaims himself King of Portugal. He marks out the boundaries of his kingdom, which have not been changed since

1250
Under the rule of Alfonso III the Moors are banished

1267
The Badajoz treaty defines the border between Spain and Portugal

1415-1560
Portugal evolves into a world power through colonization

1488
Circumnavigation of the Cape of Good Hope. Sea routes to India and China are established

1495-1521
Growth of power under Manuel I

1500
Discovery of Brazil. Spices are shipped from Asia and gold from Africa. The Asian colonies are lost. Portugal retains control of Brazil and parts of Africa

1578
King Sebastião is killed in the battle of Alcacer-Quibir, ending his campaign against the Moroccans in absolute defeat

1580
Philip II of Spain becomes King of Portugal

1640
The Duke of Bragança starts a revolution against Spanish rule and is crowned King João after his success in restoring Portuguese independence

1668
The Treaty of Lisbon recognizes Portugal's independence

1775
Earthquake destroys Lisbon, much of the Algarve and Alentejo

1910
The Republican Revolution ends the Bragança dynasty

1933
After 23 years of political and economic turmoil, António de Oliveira Salazar establishes a military dictatorship

1949
Portugal joins NATO

1968
The more liberal Marcello Caetano replaces Salazar

1974
The 'Carnation revolution'

1975
Independence of Angola and Mozambique

1976
First democratic constitution

1986
Portugal joins the EEC

1987-1995
Cavaco Silva leads first majority elected party of Portugal

1996
Socialists in control under the premiership of António Guterres and State President Jorge Sampaio

are a profusion of colour as orchids bloom in their hundreds and pools of red peonies appear underneath the carob trees. All these splendid colours and rich perfumes reach their peak in May. Then the rains stop and the heat gets more and more intense. The vegetation dries up and the ground is covered with a layer of dust. At this time of year, the Algarve is more reminiscent of North Africa, with its fiery sunsets and the beautiful colours of a hot summer dusk. The rain does not return until October, when it washes away the dust and renders the parched earth fertile again.

In the eastern Algarve, small lizards and chameleons are a common sight on the walls of houses and restaurants (where they are often employed as full time fly catchers). Falcons, buzzards, and eagles can always be seen circling in the clear blue skies, and at night owl calls echo through the air, backed by the continuous song of the cicadas. By the riverside, storks and herons forage for food, sharing their habitat with frogs and turtles, all of which suffer in the summer months when many of the natural water reserves dry up.

The Algarve covers a relatively small area, so you can explore it at a leisurely pace and still have enough time to stop and relax, and properly appreciate its beauty.

An idyllic courtyard in Tavira

From azulejos to touradas

From the melancholic fado and saudade,
to the frenetic corridinho

Algarve

When the conquering Moors first arrived from North Africa, which lies to the south-east of the Iberian peninsula, they quite logically named their new-found territory *Al Gharb,* which is Arabic for 'the West'. The Algarve was occupied by the Moors for five centuries, and not surprisingly the influence of their culture and language is still evident, particularly in the Portuguese language. The prefix 'al' for instance, is found in many words, eg *alfazema* (lavender), *alecrim* (rosemary), *almoço* (lunch)... and *azulejos* (see entry in next column).

Atlantis

Just 3 km north of Loulé lies the Cruz da Assumada valley. The philologist S. Hemerding maintained that the valley had been laid out according to precise plans and exact dimensions by the people of Atlantis — the continent said to have sunk beneath the Atlantic just south of Gibraltar —

A beautiful azulejo mosaic in the overgrown Estói Castle gardens

over 100 000 years ago. This area of dry scrubland is scattered with monumental stone formations, some of which resemble animals. Hemerding discovered a sphinx looking down from a menhir on to the expanse of land below. He also recorded 'extraordinarily high levels of energy' which he captured on his so-called 'metaphysical photographs'.

Azulejos

Public squares, park benches, fountains, even road signs, are decorated with lovely hand-painted tiles known as *azulejos*. They are as integral a part of Portuguese culture as Port itself. Made with a technique inherited from Arab craftsmen, their name does not derive from the Portuguese word for blue *(azul)* as one would expect, but from the Arab word *al-zulayi* which means a small stone.

Camões

Luís Vaz de Camões (1524-80) is one of Portugal's greatest poets, best known for his epic *The Lusiad.* Published in 1572, this poem is packed with valuable insights into Portuguese history and tradition, telling of Vasco de Gama's incredible voyage and his discovery of the East Indies.

Cão de Água

Every self-respecting fisherman once kept a *Cão de Água* (water dog) on board. A specifically Portuguese breed, not unlike a poodle, it was kept both as a pet and a talisman. It was believed that this dog could gauge the depth of water and warn of any approaching shallows, as well as picking up the scent of passing shoals of fish. Such a capable shipmate would of course be handsomely rewarded, with a payroll of fresh sardines. Some breeders are trying to reintroduce this valuable animal back on to boats.

Castles

There are at least 100 castles and monuments scattered across Portugal. Many of them date back to the period of struggle between Muslims and Christians, while others, built between the 12th and 14th centuries, such as the coastal forts of Lagos and Faro, bore witness to the great age of discovery. There are two of these historic castles which should definitely be seen: The Templars' (holy knights) castle of Castro Marim boasts a spectacular view across the river Guadiana, that forms a natural border with Andalusia; and the 10th century Silves Castle, built by the Moors – an impressive structure with its bright red battlements and towers, spacious courtyard and well-preserved drainage system. The ruined castles of Aljezur and Alcoutim also offer great views.

Chimneys

These characteristic landmarks of the province come in all shapes and sizes. Some are topped with miniature roofs, or are intricately painted and decorated with ornate motifs. Their white-washed forms stand out strongly against the cloudless blue sky. Their origin dates back to the Christian *Reconquista*. Many of the Moors were forcibly converted to Christianity, but then committed a cunning act of civil disobedience. In order to continue practising their religion, they built small minarets on the flat roofs of their houses, and circumvented objections with the claim that these were chimneys.

Churches and Monasteries

Tavira boasts the most churches of all the Algarve towns – it has over 30. At first sight they appear to be rather run down, but many deserve a closer inspection. The church of Santa Maria do Castelo holds the tomb of Dom Paio Peres Correia, master of the Holy Order of Knights of Santiago, who, in 1242, freed Tavira (the former Algarvian capital) from the Moors. Also worth a visit is the beautiful church of São Lourenço, near Almansil. The painted *azulejos* inside the church depict the life of Saint Laurence. On the road to Sagres (on the right hand side between Budens and Raposeira – **B5**) stands a 13th century chapel dedicated to the black Madonna: Nossa Senhora de Guadeloupe. Most of the churches are now locked up, due to a recent spate of thefts, but a key can usually be obtained from one of the neighbouring houses. A small tip to these

The age old thermal baths at Caldas de Monchique

voluntary caretakers (around 100 escudos) is always appreciated. The Algarve also has its own Buddhist monastery, the Mosteiro de Mú, which is set amidst the spectacular scenery of the Malhao Salir mountains.

Climate

Even though it is surrounded by the Atlantic, the south coast of Portugal enjoys more of a Mediterranean climate, with mild winters and hot summers. Summer nights are nice and cool and it's easy to get a comfortable night's sleep, unless of course the Levanter blows in from Morocco. This African wind makes the atmosphere hot and close. Sandwiched between the mountains and the sea, rainfall in the Algarve is scarce making it one of the driest regions in Portugal.

Clothes

Summer evenings can be quite fresh and it's always a good idea to carry an extra layer or light jacket with you. Daytime temperatures can get quite high, but the continuous Atlantic breeze has a pleasant cooling effect. The winter is short and has a spring-like feel to it, with occasional rain. In such conditions, natural fibres are generally better than synthetic ones.

Cork

Grown mostly in Alentejo and the Algarve, the cork oak is cultivated for its bark. This thick layer protects the tree against extreme temperatures and water loss. The bark or cork is peeled off every nine years. A highly flexible material, cork is ideal for insulation and bottle stoppers, as well as for a variety of art and craft products.

Corridinho

This energetic dance is performed by the *ranchos folclóricos* (local dance troupes) and takes a lot of stamina. The tempo of the music is rapid, and couples twirl each other around in a wild frenzy. There is much stomping of feet and flouncing of skirts. The melancholic reputation of the Portuguese is certainly not made evident in this colourful and uplifting spectacle.

Dinis I (1261-1325)

Dom Dinis came to the throne in 1279. Under his rule Portugal was transformed from an unremarkable medieval backwater into a world power. He built a fleet of trading ships, and reclaimed marshland for farming. In 1288 he established Lisbon's first university (which was later moved to Coimbra). He was a cultivated man and a great patron of the arts, hence the name of 'Poet King'.

Dogs

Stray dogs and cats can be seen roaming all over the place. They will often latch on to you and follow you around. If you are a dog-lover it can be tempting to adopt one for the duration of your holiday. This will, of course, cause you problems when the time comes to leave. Dog kennels do exist, but they operate on a charity basis, so any donations are gratefully accepted.

In the West: *Bridget Hicks, Colina Verdes 4, Bensafrim, 8600 Lagos. Tel: 767 159*

Near Faro: *Associação dos Amigos dos Animais Abandonados, Canil de São Francisco, Lilo Clauberg, Campina de Baixa, 8100 Loulé. Tel: 395 591*

Exportation

3000 years ago, the Phoenicians had already mastered the art of preserving sardines and tuna fish which they then exported. The Carthaginians and Celts soon followed suit as did the Romans, who even built roads to enable the preserved fish to be transported further afield. Today the canning and exportation of sardines is still one of Portugal's main industries.

Fado

The fado is a Portuguese folk-song, a lament that expresses *saudade*, a mood of 'indolent dreaming wistfulness'. Usually sung in a minor key, the tunes are mournful and based on such themes as homesickness, the suffering of the world, lost love and sailors far out to sea. Fados are traditionally played on a Portuguese lute and guitar, and sung by a male or female *fadista*, usually dressed in black. Its exact origins are unknown. Some say it is Arabic, others believe it has African or gypsy ancestry. The fado became popular in Portugal in the second half of the 19th century. The style in which it is sung today varies from region to region. In Lisbon it is dramatic and heartfelt while in the university town of Coimbra in the north it is light-hearted and sentimental. The traditional Algarve fado has been somewhat diluted with popular music.

Folklore

Each region has its own unique folk dance and every September groups of dancers known as *ranchos folclóricos* come to the Algarve to participate in a national dance competition. These dance troupes are a combination of young and old folk, and during the lead up to the final they can be seen performing in the evenings in certain hotels and restaurants. Ask at your hotel reception desk for details or else enquire at the local tourist information office.

Geography

Portugal, which constitutes one sixth of the Iberian peninsula, is geographically very different from its much bigger neighbour. Although the sources of its main rivers – the Minho, the Douro, the Tagus and the Guadiana – lie in Spanish soil, there are few

Freshly harvested bark from cork trees

similarities between the two peoples either side of the border. Portugal has three climate zones and an incredibly diverse landscape for a country of its size. The country itself may be small, but it boasts 835 km of Atlantic coastline, ranging from the precipitous cliffs around Cabo de São Vicente that drop 60 m into the turbulent seas below, to flat coastal areas, with calm warm seas and golden beaches, bordered by dunes and pine forests, rocks and grottoes. The Algarve is the smallest province, covering approximately 500 000 hectares. It can be subdivided into three geographical zones: the coastal zone, the limestone ridge known as the *barrocal*, and the mountain ranges of Monchique and Caldeirão. The

Fóia de Monchique at 901 m is the highest peak, with the 774 m Picota in second place. Both are extinct volcanoes. The natural hot springs in the Serra de Monchique have been renowned since Roman times for their healing properties. 500 000 litres of water spring forth daily from the Caldas de Monchique, to the benefit of those suffering from rheumatism and skin disorders. The water is also bottled and distributed in the province. The climate of the surrounding area is almost subtropical and favours an interesting mix of European and African plant life, with an abundance of trees, which provide welcome shade from the hot southern sun. On a clear day, the view from the hilltops is spectacular, stretching from Cape Vincent right along the coast as far as Lisbon.

Holy Crows

On the Cabo de São Vicente (Europe's most south-westerly point), high on the cliff top, stands a grand old lighthouse that sends its beam 100 km out to sea. According to legend, this is where St Vincent's fellow Templar knights buried him. Nobody knows the exact spot, but it is said that his funeral procession was followed by a flock of crows that kept watch over his remains. If you look up into the clear blue sky from the rocks, you will undoubtedly see these 'holy crows' circling above the cape.

Hospitality

The Algarvios are renowned for their hospitality, especially in rural areas where a local farmer will happily offer a passing hiker a glass of fresh cool water, with no questions asked. You may be offered a coffee or a shot of brandy in a bar by one of the locals, but remember that it is customary for you to then get the next round. The Portuguese are generally very friendly and like to be of service to strangers, but they don't like to be exploited! It goes without saying that it is the sociable guests who are receptive to such openness who will receive the best welcome.

Literature

Portugal's greatest literary figure, whose works have been translated into many languages, is the poet Luís Vaz de Camões (see page 11). He also wrote lyric verse, much of which is infused with *saudade*, a melancholic longing which is characteristic of the Portuguese. Portugal's most important modern writer is Fernando Pessoa (1888-1935). Born in Lisbon and raised in South Africa, he spoke both English and Portuguese. He wrote under three different names, which he called his 'heteronyms' – Alvaro do Campo, Ricardo Reis, and Alberto Caeiro – and created a biography for each one of them. Among the most acclaimed contemporary writers are José Saramago (b. 1922) whose works include *The Memorial*, *The Stone Raft*, and *Hope in Alentejo*, and António Lobo Antunes (b. 1942) who wrote *The Judas Kiss*.

The Moors

The Moors first crossed the Straits of Gibraltar in 711 AD and conquered the territory occupied by the Visigoths. These Islamic conquerors gradually became integrated with the native popula-
tion. They brought about many changes and put a workable social infrastructure in place. This part of the Iberian peninsula was dominated by the Moors until the 13th century, by which time they had left a long and lasting mark. Evidence of their civilization and influence can still be seen today in the culture and architecture of the Algarve, as well as in the physical features of the Algarvios themselves.

Nuns' breasts

Strange as it may sound, this is what the Portuguese call the snow white almond cakes, lightly flavoured with jasmine and decorated with small silver sugar balls. The rest is left to your imagination. This *doce de Algarve* is of oriental origin and found its way into the cloisters many years ago. The nuns passed the recipe down to the *senhoras de bolos* (the pastry cooks).

Peixe de aranha

The so-called 'spider fish', which brandishes a number of spikes across its back, likes to bury itself just beneath the surface of the sand. If you are unfortunate enough to tread on one, you are in for a nasty sting. Locals recommend either sucking the poison out or washing it away with vinegar. Fishermen on the other hand lay a *pedra de veneno* (another type of shellfish) over the wound, which apparently draws out the poison. If all this fails, the best thing to do is consult a doctor.

Picnics

Picnics by the river or on the beach are a Sunday ritual in which the whole family takes part. Everything you need can be bought either on the way or on location, as local farmers sell their fruit, cheese and bread by the roadside or else do the rounds at the picnic sites themselves.

Port

A fortified wine that is one of Portugal's most celebrated specialities. Port is made from grapes grown on the steep slopes of the Douro valley, near the town of Oporto. It is aged in oak casks and blended from wines of different vintages. Ruby port, a fruity wine, is aged for up to 5 years; Tawny port, pale, smooth and dry, is aged between 15 and 20 years; Vintage port, made from a single blend, is aged for 15 years or more and is sweeter, more full-bodied and deeper in colour than tawny or ruby port.

Rodovlária Nacional

The state run bus service has a wide network that links the small towns and more remote areas with the main centres. A number of private firms supplement this network. All of these transport networks operate a luxury coach service for long distance journeys between the main towns eg. Algarve-Lisbon, Coimbra-Porto.

Sardines

The Algarvios' favourite fish is traditionally grilled on charcoal fires, and its smell wafts from every alley-way, harbour, and restaurant. Portimão has the biggest fishing fleet and a fully mechanized harbour to accomodate it. The days when you could see hundreds of baskets spilling over with fish being thrown manually on to the dockside are

A typical arabesque chimney

long gone. The only place such a colourful spectacle can still occasionally be enjoyed is at the harbour of Ferragudo.

Saudade

An ancient Portuguese word that cannot be translated into any other language. It describes an intense, deep and melancholic longing for something which remains indefinable.

Shellfish

An abundance of shellfish thrives in the coastal waters of the Algarve: *Amêijoas* (cockles), *Mexilhões* (black mussels), and *Lingueirão* (a type of clam). *Búzios* are like giant whelks, whose shells are used as fog-horns at sea.

Touradas

These Portuguese bullfights are a more humane version of the Spanish Corrida, mainly because the bull is not ultimately killed. A *tourada* can last up to three hours and if you wish to see one, it is advisable to book a seat in the shade (*sombra*) or one that's half in the sun and half in the shade (*sol e sombra*) You can even get an *almofada* (cushion) from the ticket office.

Fresh from the ocean

Lobster and crab, sardines and sword fish...
there's no better place to enjoy the fruits of the sea

Sardines are the fish in most plentiful supply here. Traditionally, these plump and tasty silver fish are grilled over a charcoal fire and served with a hunk of rustic bread and a salad sprinkled with fresh thyme. Shrimps, lobsters, squid, and crabs are prepared in an equally simple fashion to maintain their fresh flavour and nutritional value. Vegetables are bought fresh every day from the local market, and most dishes are seasoned with garlic and onions which are fundamental ingredients. It is this simplicity and freshness of ingredients that make Portuguese cuisine so good.

A classic Portuguese restaurant meal would start off with the *sopa de dia* (soup of the day). Soups tend to be thick and are usually made with blended vegetables and potatoes. Other alternatives for a starter may include *caldo verde*, a hotpot made with green beans or cabbage, or a bowl of *canja de galinha* which is chicken

Simply prepared but fresh and wholesome: a typical Algarvian meal

soup served with rice and lemon slices, garnished with fresh mint.

As a rule, fish is always a wiser choice in the run-of-the-mill restaurants. Meat (especially beef) is often of a poor quality and tends to be over-cooked. There are exceptions, however, and if you do feel like eating meat, then the lamb, poultry and rabbit dishes are usually a safe bet. The Algarve speciality *frango com piri piri* is a hot spicy chicken dish well worth sampling.

Since the grapes are cultivated on the coast in a chalky, sandy soil, wine from the Algarve is characteristically full-bodied. Lagos, Lagoa, Tavira, and Portimão are the most important wine-producing regions in the province. If you prefer a lighter wine, then you should try some of the wines from the Dão or Douro regions. *Vinho verde* (green wine) is a summer wine made from young grapes that should be served well chilled. Good country wine is produced in the Alentejo region (in Borba or Reguengos for example).

Dessert usually comes in the form of a generous selection of fresh fruit. Portuguese tables are usually laden with an astonishing array of seasonal fruit: sweet grapes, fresh figs, pomegranates, *nesperas* (an edible medlar), an abundance of oranges, and various kinds of melon. Those with a real sweet tooth should try the *doces.* These very sweet pastries have a distinctly oriental flavour. Some of them come filled with a bright yellow gelatinous sweet substance known as *ovos moles.* This traditional confection is made from egg yolk and rice water, following a well-guarded recipe originally passed down from monks and nuns to subsequent generations of pastry cooks. There is another more translucent type of pastry filling known as *gila* and this, is made from a sweet pumpkin preserve.

If you want to round your meal off with coffee, try a *bica* — a small, strong espresso — and if you want to go the whole hog, order it with a glass of *medronho* or a more mature *antiqua* brandy. If you prefer decaffeinated coffee, ask for a *nescafé.* As an alternative to coffee, many Portuguese like to finish off their meal with a *chá de limão* – a small cup of hot water with a squeeze of lemon, which is supposed to freshen the palate and aid digestion.

Hot meals are eaten twice a day, but the main one is the evening meal which is normally served at around eight o'clock. Dinner is traditionally a family occasion, and that includes grandparents, uncles and aunts, nephews and nieces...

Restaurants

The more basic restaurants frequented by the locals are invariably lively places where noise levels tend to be high, as diners of all ages engage in animated conversation and compete with blaring television sets. The food in these more down to earth establishments is usually both good and cheap.

For wholesome meat and chicken dishes, try the *churrasqueiras* which specialize in charcoal-grilled food. The barbecue is usually set up by the front entrance and you can watch — and smell — your food being prepared. *Marisqueiras* on the other hand specialize in fish and shellfish, especially mussels, crayfish, lobster and crab. Here you will be supplied with a wooden board and a small hammer, perhaps even a stone, for cracking open the claws and shells. Small basins with water are thoughtfully provided for rinsing your hands.

For a quick bite to eat, the local snack bars offer a choice of salads, sandwiches (*sandes*) with *queijo* (cheese) or *fiambre* (a kind of cooked ham), and *pregos*, bread rolls filled with a piece of grilled meat or a hamburger. If you fancy something sweet, *pastelarias* serve an array of cakes and are popular meeting places for schoolchildren and old ladies alike. *Gelaterias* are equally popular and usually offer a good selection of quality ice creams and sorbets.

Alcohol

The Portuguese love a glass or two of wine with their meals. The most popular alcoholic beverages after wine are beer, port and a type of brandy known as *medronho. Aguardente de figo,* which is made from figs, and *bagaço,* from smoked wine grapes, are also potent brews. Beer is probably cheaper here than anywhere else in Europe, as the breweries are state funded. To order a large draught beer, ask for *uma caneca de cerveja* while an *uma imperial* is a small beer.

Specialities

Cataplana is a delicious speciality served in many of the coastal restaurants. It is made of ham, onions, mussels and vegetables which are all mixed together and simmered in a special tightly-sealed pot. When cooked, the pot is brought directly to your table and only then is it opened, unleashing a delicious aroma. Squid is very popular and is served in a variety of different ways. *Lulas* are small and tender, and are usually fried in butter. They can be eaten with or without their ink. *Polvos* are larger more mature squid, usually served Spanish style, in battered rings. The spicy *Polvo recheado* is squid stuffed with tomatoes, onions, eggs, and bread. One of the principal Algarvian staples is, of course, the sardine. This is normally charcoal grilled and served on a slice of bread accompanied with a green salad. *Pescada,* another national favourite, is whiting served with salted potatoes, green beans, and a hard boiled egg, traditionally seasoned with vinegar and olive oil at the table. *Bacalhau* (cod) is so popular that there are 365 recipes for it – one for each day of the year. *Bife de atum* (tuna fish steak) has a meat-like consistency and is delicious with fried onions. *Espadarte* (sword fish steak) is a local speciality which many maintain is far superior to salmon. When smoked (*fumado*) it makes a tasty

Sardines are usually charcoal grilled

starter. Going back to the soups, an absolute must is the *sopa à alentejana*, a hearty garlic broth complemented with a poached egg and a sprinkling of coriander, and best enjoyed when dipped with bread. *Bife à portuguesa* is a somewhat tough thin slice of beef fried in a ceramic pan and marinated in wine, oil, bay leaves, and garlic. It is then topped with ham, a fried egg, and served with fried potatoes. A traditional summer dish is *leitão* – suckling pig roasted with thyme and served cold. *Chouriços assados* are pork sausages richly flavoured with paprika and garlic. They are flame grilled with a strong brandy and the drips of fat are collected to make a tasty sauce, which is best enjoyed mopped up on a piece of bread.

Breakfast

Evening meals are substantial and breakfast is therefore a frugal affair. It traditionally consists of *café com leite* (white coffee), *galão* (another type of milky coffee), or a cup of sweet hot chocolate, with *torrada* (toast buttered on both sides).

Ceramics, porcelain, copper and cork

Traditional arts and crafts are still very much alive

Deep in the heart of the Algarvian countryside, time seems to have stood still. Local produce is still used as payment for goods. A farmer might exchange some of his oranges for a red cabbage or two from his neighbour's farm. A dozen eggs might be given in return for a basket of green beans, while the village doctor would be happy enough to accept a sack of potatoes as payment for consultation. This currency system is obviously not one that can be adopted by outsiders. But don't worry, your cash will be readily accepted. It is ill-advised, however, to attempt to barter as prices are fixed. If you are set on a big spending spree and want to be sure of getting the best value for money, then you would do well to shop around. As a general rule, the village shops are usually cheaper than the town shopping centres.

Folk art

Traditional arts and crafts are still widely practised here, often independently of the tourist industry. You can still see women sitting in front of their houses busy lace-making, knitting, embroidering and even weaving. Palm leaves and rushes (*esparto*) are among the most popular raw materials used, and in the month of May the long blades of grass can be seen everywhere as they are laid out to dry. The women of Loulé excel in the art of making straw hats and fans while around Albufeira, in Vila Real de Santo António and in the Monchique hills, local artisans specialize in transforming the same material into containers of varying sizes, table mats and floor coverings.

Basket weaving is traditionally undertaken by the men. Bamboo and willow is used in their construction; the towns of Alcoutim, Castro Marim, Odeleite, and Aljezur are particularly renowned for their craftsmanship .

Ceramics and pottery are hand-thrown and fired in Loulé, Tavira, and Moncarapacho, and painted in a typically naïve style.

The Algarvios are also skilled woodcarvers: Aljezur is famous for its intricately carved ladles,

A village souvenir shop selling handicrafts from all over Portugal

In the Marco Polo Spirit

Marco Polo was the first true world traveller. He travelled with peaceful intentions forging links between the East and the West. His aim was to discover the world, and explore different cultures and environments without changing or disrupting them. He is an excellent role model for the 20th-century traveller. Wherever we travel we should show respect for other peoples and the natural world.

WWF

while in Loulé you can find some lovely rustic wooden toys with moving parts: cyclists that pedal, birds that flap their wings, hens that peck corn... for a varied selection, visit the markets at Loulé and Faro (in the old town).

Loulé is also reputed for its hand-crafted copper and brass. This is where the best *cataplanas* are said to be made. A *cataplana* is a wok-shaped cooking pot, forerunner of the pressure cooker, used in traditional Portuguese cooking. The local smiths also turn their skilled hands to lanterns, lamps, candle holders, and solid cooking pots specially crafted for use over open fires. Particularly popular are their balcony railings, wrought into flamboyant designs. Among other hand-made goods you can find in this productive town are snug sheepskin slippers and, somewhat less practical, donkey harnesses decorated with mirror pieces and coloured tassles, purported to protect both rider and animal from the evil eye.

Flax and wool weavers are always hard at work in Monchique and Tavira, making beautiful bed covers and clothes. Azulejo tiles are made in the old workshops, and then painted with traditional age-old designs. You will be certain to see many beautiful examples of this unique art. Tiles can be made to order, but bear in mind that they are not suitable for outside walls in colder climates, as they have a tendency to crack in winter frosts.

Handicrafts from all over Portugal find their way to the Algarve. Exotic embroidery from the Madeira islands can be bought, but for a price. The brightly coloured Arraiolos carpet has been made in Alentejo for centuries, according to the same cross-stitch method inspired by Moorish design. These wonderful artefacts are both beautiful and durable.

Doces

These traditional sweets can be found everywhere. They are made from figs, almonds, eggs and honey, and formed into fruit or animal shapes. No festive table is complete without them.

Porcelain

You will see an abundance of kitsch china objects on the shelves of many a souvenir shop, but if you look in the right places, high quality porcelain can be found. The Vista Alegre factory, founded in 1824, produces some wonderful porcelain and crystal pieces, invariably designed by Italian craftsmen.

24

Ceramics

Locally made ceramic objects range from simple rustic designs to highly elaborate pieces based on original 17th and 18th century models. All kinds of plates, jugs, bowls, vases and cups are painted with colourful patterns and pictures. If you come across a bowl that looks like an upside down hat with yellow spots, it will have been made in Barcelos in north Portugal. This region is a major centre for ceramics, especially renowned for its Mexican-style figurines that can be lit from the inside and, of course, for the *galo*, the painted cockerel which is Portugal's emblem. For a small but fun souvenir, why not pick up a bird-call whistle. These are, in fact, still used today by shepherds.

Cork

From this flexible material, salad bowls, ladles, place mats, picture frames and ornate boxes are conjured up in many forms.

Portugal's lucky charm

Music

There are numerous recordings of the *ranchos folclóricos* available on CD, cassette and even vinyl. The best-selling fado singer is Amália Rodrigues, but there is an abundant choice of recordings by other fado artists. Cesária Evora, a singer of Angolan origin, is also worth a listen. Most music outlets also stock a wide selection of Brazilian music.

Jewellery

Gypsy earrings and gold filigree brooches based on traditional designs are widespread. For good quality jewellery you are better off going to the specialist shops, although you might find the occasional nice piece on the market.

Shoes

Portugal has a thriving shoe industry. Some excellent quality shoes are made here, and they are sold alongside other international brands. Prices tend to be quite reasonable.

Pewter

Not cheap, but of irreproachable quality, the pewter objects made here are worked in such a way as to resemble old silver.

Opening times

Mon–Fri: 09.00–13.00 and 15.00–19.00 hrs, Sat until 13.00 hrs.

The big supermarkets, village grocers and the shops in the tourist areas stay open all weekend. Some of the bigger shopping centres stay open all day from 10.00–21.00 hrs. The outdoor markets only trade from Monday to Saturday, except for those in Faro, Olhão and Albufeira, which have big Sunday markets.

Fireworks and flower battles

The Algarvian Festa is where the sacred and the profane combine in a unique celebration

PUBLIC HOLIDAYS

1 January: New Year's Day *(Ano Novo)*

February/March: Shrove Tuesday *(Carnaval)*

March/April: Easter *(Pascoa)*

25 April: Liberation Day; end of the 1974 Revolution *(Dia de Liberdade)*

1 May: Labour Day *(Dia Internacional do Trabalhador)*

May/June: Corpus Christi *(Corpo de Deus)*

10 June: Portugal Day *(Dia do Portugal)*; *Dia de Camões* (anniversary of the poet's death)

15 August: Assumption *(Assunção de Nossa Senhora)*

5 October: Republic Day *(Dia da República)*

1 November: All Saints' Day *(Todos os Santos)*

1 December: Restoration Day *(Restauração Portuguesa)*; end of Spanish rule in 1640

8 December: Immaculate Conception *(Imaculada Conceição da Nossa Senhora)*

Fêtes and folk festivals: year round celebrations infused with tradition

Mary is the patron saint of Portugal.

25 December: Christmas Day *(Dia do Natal)*

Portugal is a predominantly Catholic nation. Holy feast days are, however, more closely adhered to in the north than in the south. Christmas and Easter are celebrated only on one day.

Foreign embassies and consulates are closed on their corresponding national holidays as well as on the day after Christmas and Easter.

Festivals and fairs

The Portuguese *festas* are joyous and raucous occasions, when the air crackles with the sound of fireworks and bangers. Many an event is used as a pretext for celebration: the beginning of spring; the feast day of a patron saint; the anniversary of a historical figure; the blessing of a church or monument... The sound of gunfire in the early hours of the morning wakes the sleeping celebrants and announces the opening of the *festa*, which ends equally noisily with a spectacular midnight firework display.

MARCO POLO SELECTION: FESTIVALS

1 Festa da Grande Fonte
Flower festival and communal picnic by the natural springs in Alte (page 29)

2 Folk Dance Festival
Dance groups – *ranchos folclóricos* – from all over Portugal demonstrate their skills and show off their colourful costumes in a nationwide competition (page 29)

3 Carnival
Colourful and imaginative floats parade the streets of Loulé to the sounds of the Samba (page 28)

In rural areas *feiras* are held on a regular basis. There is a country fair in Moncarapacho, near Olhão, for example, that takes place on the first Sunday of every month, followed on the next Sunday by one in Estói. Other towns hold their fêtes on more specific dates (enquire at the local tourist information office for details). These *feiras* offer for sale a wide range of hand-made goods and local produce: pottery, clothes, riding gear, sturdy leather boots etc. Live-stock – sheep, corn-fed chickens, even donkeys – are also sold here. There is never any shortage of tempting food stalls, and if you're feeling peckish why not tuck into a plate of barbecued squid, a regular favourite at fairs. The din of voices bartering and advertising wares carries through the clouds of smoke that emanate from the hot cooking fat, and mingles with music from nearby bars. All these elements combine to create a perfect country fair atmosphere.

Music also plays an important part in the annual celebrations. May and June are the key months in the Algarve festive calendar when local orchestras, together with international musicians, participate in a big music festival. The National Ballet and the Gulbenkian company tour the region, and local fire brigade bands strike up in the towns and villages. Performances will usually start at 9 pm, or sometimes even later.

February

★ ✪ ☦ *Loulé Carnival.* Locals and tourists gather together to admire the colourful procession floats and dance along to pulsating Brazilian music.

The *Moncarapacho Carnival,* though not as well known, is equally animated and is held to celebrate the arrival of the almond blossoms.

Salir holds a special festival in honour of its corn – the *Festa das Espigas,* which coincides with the Sausage festival, during which enormous quantities of food and drink are consumed.

The 2nd Sunday after Easter

✪ The *Loulé Romaria* (pilgrimage) lasts for three days. First the church is blessed and then the statue of Our Lady of Piety (Senhora da Piedade) is carried by the pilgrims in a procession called the *Mãe Soberana* to a chapel at the top of a mountain. This solemn procession is followed by a lively folk festival.

1 May

★ ☼ *Festa da Grande Fonte* in Alte. This traditional festival celebrates the healing powers of the town's spring. A communal picnic is held at its source and the coming of spring is also celebrated with garlands of flowers and folkloric displays.

May/June

The Algarve Music Festival. The programme and venues are publicized well in advance.

13 June

The feast of St Antony. As well as being patron saint of the regional capital, Faro, St. Antony is also the protector of those wishing to marry. To make sure that he will not forget them, the young unmarried girls of the town will bombard the statue of the saint with flowers and pebbles on this day.

Carnival procession in Silves

August

Beer festival at the castle of Silves.

September

★ ☼ This folk dance festival is a major cultural event. Dance troupes come from all over Portugal to compete for the prestigious prize. Eliminating rounds take place throughout the province, and the finals are held in *Praia da Rocha* in *Portimão*.

Chimneys or minarets?

In the fifteenth century, the zealous King João I and his troops invaded the Moorish kingdom of Al-Gharb and set about the brutal 'christianization' of its inhabitants. Under his rule the resident 'infidels' (devout Muslims) had to either convert or be banished. They were forced to submit and were ostensibly converted. That is to say, they went through the motions of christian ritual. During this period an increasing number of round towers appeared on the flat roofs of Moorish houses. The residents maintained that these were chimneys. In the evenings, however, families would gather on the rooftops and pray to Mecca in front of what in fact were minarets. These beautifully designed and embellished 'chimneys' not only served a religious purpose, but they soon became a popular decorative feature of the otherwise plain square houses. They are now a widespread and unique architectural feature of the Algarve.

A BRIEF VISIT

The city of Lisbon and its one million inhabitants are spread across seven hills that lie along the banks of the River Tagus. It is very different in character from the rest of Portugal. At once elegant and shabby, peaceful and noisy, modern and unbelievably old-fashioned, traditional yet forward-thinking — it is a place full of contradiction and fascination.

VIEWS OF THE CITY

If you approach Lisbon from the south you will cross the *Ponte de 25 Abril,* the highest and longest suspension bridge in Europe. The view of the Portuguese capital from this impressive structure is exceptional. The Cristo Rei statue that stands guard over the bridge was built in 1938, and is a small replica of the statue of Christ that watches over Rio de Janeiro in Brazil. The bridge marks a dividing line between the Tagus estuary to the west and the rough waters of the Mar de Palha to the east.

The finest view of the city is undoubtedly the one seen from the ☙ *Castelo de São Jorge.* Here, an attractive town plan made of hand-painted tiles has been erected for the benefit of tourists. You can admire the view in the company of white peacocks that strut along the fortification walls, and the flocks of ravens that circle and caw above the ruins. The walk up to the castle will take you through the Alfama district, where the Moors originally settled. If you don't feel like walking, however, you can catch the number 37 bus which runs from

Rossio. The view from above the *Parque Eduardo VII* in the ☙ *Rua Marquês de Fronteira* extends the length of the elegant Avenida de Liberdade as far as the Praça do Comércio and the river beyond. Another fine panorama can be enjoyed from the cable car that runs from the *Praça dos Restauradores* up to the *Miradouro de São Pedro de Alcântara* which encompasses the Castelo de São Jorge and the Alfama district below.

SIGHTSEEING

The *Alfama* is Lisbon's oldest district. Its labyrinth of winding streets, interconnected with steep stone steps, are lined with ancient narrow houses. Washing hangs from the windows, adding a splash of colour, complemented by geraniums and amaryllises that sprout from tin cans and plastic pots. As you wander from one tree-shaded square to the next, you'll hear the sound of canaries in full song echoing through the houses, backed by the chorus of playing children and the occasional cry of a fishwife selling the day's catch, and catch wafts of all sorts of unfamiliar smells — olive oil mixed with diesel, orange blossoms and coffee. The Moorish atmosphere prevails as you climb on up to the *Castelo.* On the way, you will pass before the cathedral (*Sé de Sto António*) and the Casa dos Bicos on the *Avenida Infante Dom Henrique.* The stones that make up the façade of this renaissance palace have been hewn like diamonds. Today the building is used as a cultural centre and often hosts exhibitions. Just up the road is the king's fountain (*Chafriz d'El-Rei*) that spurts water from six different outlets, each of which represents one of the six social strata. Stop for breath on the esplanade of the ✹ *Igreja de Santa Luzia*, and enjoy the view across the dilapidated roof-tops of the old town to the harbour. The church itself contains some interesting azulejos, painted with scenes depicting the *Praça do Comércio* that reveal how it looked before the earthquake which struck the town in the 18th century. Further fine examples of this 16th century art form can be found in the *Igreja de São Roque* on the *Praça Trindade Coelho*. It can be reached by cable car from the *Praça dos Restauradores*. This church also contains the sumptuous chapel of John the Baptist (*João Baptiste*). Decorated with alabaster, marble, lapis lazuli, gold and silver, it bears witness to Portugal's former affluence.

The *Torre de Belém* is an imposing monument that stands in the heart of the Belém district. It was erected in 1521 to commemorate the nation's maritime heroes. The nearby *Padrão dos Descobrimentos* monument is dedicated to the country's great explorers, while the impressive *Mosteiro dos Jerónimos* opposite is a real masterpiece of 16th-century Manueline architecture. This is where both Vasco da Gama and Camões are buried. The garden enclosed by the cloister is a pretty and peaceful place.

Just next door on the *Praceta de Afonso de Albuquerque* stands the *Museo Nacional dos Coches* (Coach Museum) that houses a splendid collection of luxury carriages dating from the 17th to the 19th century. From here you can catch a tram to the town centre (numbers 15 and 16). The route runs along the river Tagus to the heart of the city – the *Praça do Comércio* esplanade. This is where foreign ships arriving in Lisbon weighed anchor in full view of the King's palace which once dominated the square overlooking the docks. The *Bairro da Lapa* rises up from the banks of the Tagus. During the 18th and 19th century, many of the nobility built their luxury manors and villas upon this hill. These faded pink palaces are now once grand town houses are now occupied mainly by embassies and wealthy businesses. Lilacs and bougainvillaea cascade over the walls to complete the idyllic scene. The nearby *Chiado* quarter is an up-market district. Partly destroyed by fire in 1989 the luxury shops and buildings were systematically renovated and the area has retained its elegance. The *Santa Justa Elevador* (lift) on the *Rua de Ouro* links the upper town to the lower town.

The *Convento do Carmo* which was partly destroyed in the 1755 earthquake has been left in its semi-ruined state as a memorial to the tragic event. The fact that the structure is roofless lends a special atmosphere to the exhibitions and performances held in the nave. Lisbon's real showpiece, the *Avenida da Liberdade* was built in 1882 in imitation of the Champs-Elysées. Sadly, it is now choked with traffic and the proud old buildings that once lined the town's main artery are giving way to an increasing number of ugly modern office buildings. The central pedestrian reservation paved with Calçada mosaics is still an interesting place to stroll along. Tall leafy trees, splashing

Interpreting gestures

If you see someone tugging enthusiastically at his or her ear, it means that they are impressed with something or that something good has just happened. If it's something really spectacular, then the hand reaches over the head and tugs at the opposite ear, a gesture usually accompanied by the words: *E assim!*

fountains, old fashioned kiosks, and weathered park benches, take your mind off the hustle and bustle for a while.

MUSEUMS

Museu Arqueológico
Gives a good overview of Portugal's history, and displays many prehistoric artefacts.
Tue-Sun 10.00-17.00 hrs; by the Convento do Carmo

Museu das Janelas Verdes
The real name of this museum, the most renowned one in Lisbon, is the *Museu Nacional de Arte Antiga*. Its treasures include tapestries from the 17th and 18th century, and works of art by such masters as Cranach, Velázquez, Dürer, Fragonard, and Raphael, as well as many fine examples of azulejos and porcelain.
Tue, Wed, Fri, Sat 10.00-17.00 hrs, Thurs and Sun 10.00-19.00 hrs; Rua das Janelas Verdes

RESTAURANTS

On the whole the restaurants in Lisbon, whether large or small, are of a good quality and reasonably priced. The following establishments are recommended:

Pap' Açorda
◉ Bairro Alto's most popular restaurant. A house speciality is the *Açorda,* made with crab and coriander. Reservation is a must.
Rua da Atalaia 57-59; Tel: 346 48 11; Category 1

O Polícia
◉ One of the best places for authentic, quality Portuguese cuisine. The fish is extra fresh and the wine list excellent. It's always packed at lunchtime, but in the evenings you'll find it a little calmer.
Avenida Conde de Valbom 125; Tel: 796 35 05; Category 2

Trindade
⚘ Formerly a monastery, this *cervejaria* is a popular meeting place among the locals. It stays open until the early hours and is a good spot to round the evening off with a nightcap, or for a midnight snack such as king prawns or mussels. Beer is the most popular drink here, but wine is available on request.
Rua Nova da Trindade 20; Tel: 342 33 56; Category 2

SHOPPING

Centro Comercial Amoreiras
⚘ Lisbon's biggest and most spectacular shopping centre is an architectural overstatement. Pink and yellow, with postmodern elements, black mirrored windows, and an Arabic flavour to boot, it towers up to

challenge the city landscape. It has to be seen to be believed and the shops stay open until late.
Avenida Engenheiro Duarte Pacheco/ Rua da Mota Pinto

Chiado

Lisbon's up-market shopping district is in the upper city. Can be reached via the *Santa Justa lift,* on the *Rua do Ouro.*

Lisbon offers a wide range of accommodation, from top international hotels to basic pensions.

Albergaria Senhora do Monte

Well-appointed hotel in the old town, with extensive views of the city and its castles.
28 rooms; Calçada do Monte 39; Tel: 886 60 02; Category 2

York House Residência

Despite the name, this stylish hotel, formerly a 16th century monastery, is well and truly Portuguese in character. Next to the Museu Nacional de Arte Antiga. Reservations recommended.
32 rooms; Rua das Janelas Verdes 32; Tel: 396 24 35; Category 1

Bars

One of the city's trendiest hangouts is the ✤ ⚡ *Pavillão Chinês (Rua Dom Pedro 89).* A good venue for Afro-Brazilian music is ⚡ *Pé Sujo* in the Alfama district. *Banana Power (Rua Fradesso da Silveira 25)* is classy, but rather snobbish and frequented by Lisbon's jet-set. The current 'in' club is ⚡ the *Alcântara Café (Rua Maria Luísa Holstein 15).* The décor is minimal and it's technically sophisticated. Complete with a dining area under palm trees. *(For table reservations, Tel: 362 12 26).* The disco doesn't start until midnight at the earliest.

Cafés

Cafés are the social hub of the city. The most famous are the *Suiça* in Rossio, which serves a great breakfast on the terrace, and the *Brasileira* on the *Largo do Chiado* where poets, artists, and journalists have gathered for over a century.

Turismo-Palácio Foz

Summer 09.00-20.00 hrs; Praça dos Restauradores; Tel: 346 33 14

Calçada Mosaico

Mosaic paving is a unique Portuguese art, one that is particularly prevalent in Lisbon. After the earthquake of 1755, many of the paths and walkways of the city were repaved with grey, black and white stones arranged in pictorial images, imaginative patterns and geometric designs. If you look down as you walk across these beautifully paved streets you will see some lovely images of galleons sailing proudly through rolling waves, meandering rivers, and carpets of flowers in front of park benches. Elsewhere the bottoms of trees are encircled in black rings. Sadly the number of practicing *calceteiros* — craftsmen skilled in this exacting art — is fast diminishing.

Rolling dunes and blue lagoons

Abandoned palaces, Roman mosaics and the
Ria Formosa Nature Reserve

Faro, the regional capital, lies on the border between two distinct sub-regions of the Algarve: Sotavento — the sandy Algarve — to the east of Faro, stretches as far as the Spanish border, while Barlavento — the rocky Algarve — is a long coastal strip to the west, scored with hidden coves, natural bays and spectacular rock formations. The long, flat beaches of Sotavento and the warmer waters make this an ideal pace for families with children to spend their holidays. Just beyond the suburbs of Faro, a long stretch of marshland extends eastwards for miles. A large part of this area is a protected nature reserve known as the *Reserva Natural da Ria Formosa*. The Sotavento lagoons have a character all of their own. Their mud banks may look smooth and inviting, but the silt is thick and deep, so a walk across them is not really recommended. Unless, of course, you want to roll up your trousers, just as the local fishermen do, who come here to dig for the plentiful shellfish.

Castro Marim, a sleepy, picturesque town with a colourful past

---

Hotel and restaurant prices

Hotels
Category L: over £100
Category 1: £70–£100
Category 2: £40–£70
Category 3: under £40

Restaurants
Category L: over £20
Category 1: £13–£20
Category 2: £7–£13
Category 3: under £7

The above prices are for one night in a double room with breakfast included.

Prices for a full meal including starter, main course, dessert and a drink. Telephone numbers are not listed for restaurants where only Portuguese is spoken.

CASTRO MARIM

(M4) ⭐ This area is made up of a unique combination of geographical features: to the east runs the Guadiana River, while in the west and north lie the dry and barren Mato mountains, all interspersed with salt marshes and lagoons. It is an unearthly, glimmering landscape. In the midst of it all is the peaceful town of Castro Marim, one of the oldest and historically most interesting settlements in southern Portugal. The two ruined fortresses which dominate the town were originally built to defend the access routes to Spain. It was King Alfonso III who, in the 13th century, transformed the Moorish castle into a well-defended garrison fort that guarded the region.

Today, the ancient castle houses the main offices of the *Reserva Natural do Sapal de Castro Marim*, a wildlife park that covers around 2000 hectares in which a diversity of flora and fauna thrive. The employees of the nature reserve are responsible for the protection of these indigenous species. A small archaeological museum is also housed in the castle and displays objects unearthed in the area. The walls of the 17th century Forte de São Sebastião are impressive. The sheer size of these ramparts, together with the position of the fortress, which stood at the junction of two busy Roman roads, would have been enough to scare off the boldest of invaders.

The nearby *Ponte da Senhora dos Milagres* was once a gathering place for pilgrims. This bridge held a special significance, as the ash tree that grew next to it was believed to possess healing powers. At the end of their pilgrimage, the participants would congregate here and cut a branch — a *ramo do freixa* — from the tree, which they would hang in their homes in the belief that it would protect their families from ill health.

On 15 August Castro Marim holds its annual festival of ✪ *São Bartolomeu* in the castle grounds. It is a popular celebration and you can find a selection of locally made wickerwork items for sale. *Access to the castle is from the Rua do Castelo. Access to the Forte de São Sebastião is from the Rua José Alves Moreira.*

Coastal landscape of Faro

SURROUNDING AREA

Alcoutim   (L2)

★ The road which goes north from Castro Marim towards the Alentejo region follows the same route as the ancient Roman road and runs parallel to the Guadiana river. The atmosphere that reigns over the surrounding landscape, which is largely uninhabited, is still and silent. The small and peaceful village of Alcoutim lies 35 km north of Castro Marim along this road. It boasts a rich history and among its illustrious inhabitants were Fernando I of Portugal and Henrique II of Castile, who lived here during the late 14th century. Both are buried in the castle where, today, art exhibitions and displays of archaeological excavations are frequently held. Alcoutim's harbour was once graced with the presence of pioneering galleons and

the great ships of the Phoenicians, Greeks and Carthaginians. A stroll through the village alleyways is equally fascinating, and a visit to one of the bars along the way, to sample some freshly caught river eels, is recommended. Alcoutim also has a lovely parish church with a Renaissance portal and Holy Communion shrine made of silver and mother of pearl. There is a spectacular view ⬇ from the top of the castle ruins across the roof-tops of the whitewashed houses to the neighbouring town of Sanlúcar de Guadiana which is just across the border. With its own historic castle and colourful fishing boats, this Spanish town is in many ways similar to its Portugese counterpart. But although Spain and Portugal are actually only a stone's throw apart, in many other ways they are worlds apart.

Martim Longo   (K3)

A further 30 km into the mountains is the charming village of Martim Longo which is worth a visit. It is said to be more characteristic of the Alentejo region than the Algarve, but it is a perfect starting point for excursions into the surrounding hills. The area is very isolated and you'll come across more buzzards and eagles than fellow hikers.

FARO

(16) The main international airport serving the Algarve is in Faro. Every summer, holidaymakers from all over the world land here by the thousand. On a quest for the Portuguese sun and sand, the large majority head straight for the coastal resorts. The Algarvian capital itself has unfortunately lost much of its former charm. Many of its classical buildings were destroyed by the earthquake which struck in 1755. The Cidade Velha (the old town), however, still retains something of its old world atmosphere. Within the boundary walls stands the former Dominican Convent, now a museum which provides an interesting overview of the town's history.

Before the Phoenicians and Greeks arrived and established a trading centre, Faro was no more than a small fishing village. Some 2000 years ago, the Romans built a large harbour here, but it remained largely unused. It wasn't really until 712 AD that the Moors began to develop the area. It attained the official status of a town in 1540 and was elevated to the rank of episcopal seat of the Algarve thirty years later. In 1596 the town was besieged by the Earl of Essex and much of it was burned down. Shortly after the great earthquake of 1755, Faro was named the official capital of the Algarve. Disaster struck again when Napoleon brutally attacked the city in 1808. Despite its turbulent history, however, Faro has an unruffled quality, which lends it a certain charm. With a population of 30 000, it is the region's administrative centre and still holds the episcopal seat. Economically it is thriving, thanks to an established fish processing industry, salt extraction plant, and various businesses manufacturing cork goods.

On the outskirts of the town is the Praia de Faro, the nearest beach, on a spit of sand known as the Ilha de Faro. There is a bridge connecting it to the mainland or alternatively it can be reached by boat (departures from the *bombeiros* — fire station). Unfortunately, the ship that once sailed to Africa from here no longer operates a service due to lack of demand.

SIGHTSEEING

Old town

Behind the pretty little marina and the *Jardim Manuel Bivar* park with its blue and white striped Café Pavilion, stands the *Arco da Vila*, an ornate Baroque gateway that leads into the old town — ★ *Cidade Velha.* Storks can often be seen nesting upon it and the white marble statue of St Thomas Aquinas is the unfortunate target of their droppings. The old town is well preserved. Its beautiful patrician houses stand proudly on cobbled streets that lead to an imposing square containing the Sé Cathedral, Bishop's Palace and former orphanage. Right at the end of the square is Faro's town hall. In the late summer the shady orange trees that line the square are laden with fruit which may

38

Thomas of Aquinas watches over the Arco da Vila in Faro

Above the altar is a gold-leafed wood carving of the *Last Supper* that dates back to the 16th century. Eighteenth century azulejos decorate the *Capela das Almas. Largo de São Pedro*

Nossa Senhora do Carmo. A two-towered Baroque church with a rather macabre Chapel of Bones in its garden, which has a whole wall covered with human skulls and bones. Visitors are greeted by a charming inscription that says: 'Consider: one day you too will look like this'. *Largo do Carmo*

The Bishop's Cathedral known simply as *Sé* was built in 1251. Originally of Romanesque-Gothic design, over the centuries it underwent various alterations and additions and it displays a curious mixture of Gothic, Renaissance and Baroque styles. The chapel is tiled with 18th century blue and white azulejos. On Friday afternoons, you can listen to the red *chinoiserie* organ being played. From the ⬇ clock tower there is a fine view over the town and coastline. *Largo da Sé*

look tempting to pick, but are bitter and inedible.

On the town's second square, the *Largo Dom Alfonso III*, stand the *Archaeological Museum* and the *Municipal Library,* which are housed in the old monastery. In the alley behind the square, *Porta da Moura* exhibits good quality handicrafts from the Algarve. (*Daily; Rua do Repouso 5*)

Churches

The *Igreja de São Francisco* is a single-naved church built in the 16th century. It was devastated in the earthquake of 1755, but you can still see some fine azulejos on the walls and ceiling along with many gilded wood carvings. There is a small museum annexed to the church, displaying sacred art and prehistoric findings. *Largo de São Francisco*

The *Igreja de São Pedro* was built in the mid-16th century on the foundations of a hermitage.

MUSEUMS

Museu Arqueológico e Lapidar Infante de Henrique

This archaeological museum displays prehistoric finds unearthed in and around Faro with Roman mosaics from Milreu, as well as paintings and other sacred artworks. The old cloister boasts a beautiful Renaissance interior. *Tue-Sun 10.00-12.00 and 14.00-17.00 hrs; Largo Dom Alfonso III*

Museu Etnológico

Displays based on local crafts and industries, regional art and reconstructed interiors of the Algarvian

houses of yester-year.
Mon-Fri 09.30-12.30 and 14.00-17.30 hrs; Praça Alexandre Herculano

Museu Marítimo Ramalho Ortigão

This museum is dedicated to the different fishing methods practised along the Algarvian coast. Lots of models of old boats, including a replica of Vasco da Gama's ship, the *São Gabriel*.
Mon-Fri 09.30-12.30 and 14.00-17.30 hrs, Sat 09.00-13.00 hrs; in the yacht harbour behind the Hotel Eva, in the port authority building.

CAFÉS & RESTAURANTS

Café Aliança

❖ A spacious, well-established café where the locals begin and end their day. A great place to sit with a *bica* (strong espresso) and watch the world go by.
Rua Dr. Francisco Gomes and Rua de Santo António (two entrances)

Cidade Velha

Next to the cathedral, this small, elegant restaurant serves good, imaginative cuisine and excellent wine.
Rua Domingos Guiero 19; Tel: 271 45; Category 1

Clube Naval

An ideal retreat for a sundowner on the terrace. Worth a visit for the fine view of the harbour across the tops of the palm trees. The food isn't bad, though the service is somewhat indifferent.
Behind Marina, 2nd floor; Category 2

Pastelaria Gardy

❖ Right in the middle of the pedestrian zone, this is a popular meeting place for people of all ages, who come here to see and

be seen. An ideal place to stop for coffee and cake.
Rua de Santo António

Green's

Not much room, but the service is excellent. Shellfish, grilled steaks and good wines.
Daily (except Sun); Largo do Pé da Cruz 9-11 (back entrance in the big car park); Tel: 21303; Category 1

Sousa

❖ A good traditional restaurant with a variety of fish and meat dishes prepared in the typical Portuguese way.
Entrance through a little bar at the front; Largo do Pé da Cruz 41; Category 2

On l'Ilha de Faro

Camané

Small restaurant right at the tip of the Ilha de Faro. Specialities are fish, and an extraordinary almond soup. Reservation essential.
Daily (except Mon); Praia de Faro (left after the bridge); Tel: 817 539; Category 1

SHOPPING

The *Rua de Santo António* and the alley-ways leading off it form a pedestrianized shopping zone lined with boutiques, shoe shops, and souvenir shops selling good quality ceramics, pewter and other handicrafts.

For a wide selection of practical and well-made products from the Serra do Caldeirão, visit the *Casa da Serra* in the shopping centre opposite the big market hall.
Mon-Fri 09.30-13.00 and 14.00-19.00, Sat 10.00-13.00 hrs; Rua Justino Cúmano/Praça d'Alandra

HOTELS

Faro
Opposite the yacht harbour with sun terrace on the roof.
52 rooms; Praça D. Francisco Gomes 2; Tel: 803 279; Category 2

Madalena
A clean and friendly pension in the centre of town.
22 rooms; Rua Conselheiro Bivar 109; Tel: 805 806/07; Category 3

Mónaco
A three star hotel between the airport and the town. Provides free transport into town and to the beach.
Montenegro; Tel: 818 106, Fax: 818 923; Category 2-3

CHRISTMAS CRIBS

As Portugal is a Catholic country, the street Christmas decorations are centred around the nativity scene. At the beginning of advent, Christmas cribs appear in towns and villages all over the Algarve. The biggest and most elaborate nativity scenes are traditionally created by the local fire brigade. Painted figures are set in a lovingly created landscape, complete with twinkling stars and cascading waterfalls. The Faro *bombeiros* are renowned for their imaginative cribs.
Next to the marina

INFORMATION

Posto de Turismo
Mon-Fri 09.00-12.30 and 14.00-17.00 hrs; Rua da Misericórdia (left of the Arco da Vila); Tel: 803 604

OLHÃO

(K 5-6) Ten kilometres east of Faro is Olhão, the largest fishing port in the Algarve. It lies by a lagoon and encompasses the two sandbank islands of Armona and Culatra that can be reached by a regular ferry boat service. This rather curious town would seem more at home in the deserts of North Africa, with its labyrinth of twisting streets and interconnecting alley-ways, randomly scattered with *açoteias*. These striking whitewashed cubic houses with their flat terraced roofs are unique to the area. This style of architecture originated from Africa and their design is rooted in practicality: the white paint keeps the houses cool during the day, while at night the flat roofs capture the cool sea breeze, and one can sleep here when the heat becomes too oppressive. Up until the 18th century, Olhão was nothing more than a stopover for fishermen forced to wait out bad storms. Today it has a population of 25 000, making it the second largest town of the province.

A morning tipple

Para matar a bicho is the toast an Algarvian makes at breakfast time when chasing a morning coffee (*bica*) with a shot of brandy. Roughly translated it means 'to kill off the bacteria' and is a saying that is believed to originate from the time when plague was rife. Used in a modern context, it is a convenient way to justify a morning tipple.

Abundant catches of carp, bass, sardines, perch and anchovies are unloaded along its quays. The large freshwater lake, enclosed within a natural sand spit, is shaped like an eye, hence the town's name, which is a contraction of *olho d'agua,* meaning 'eye of water'.

Olhão owes its prosperity to the astuteness and cunning of the local fishermen. In 1799 the English were fighting the Spanish, and both their harbours, in Gibraltar and Cadiz, had officially been closed to visiting ships. But the clever fishermen of Olhão defied orders, and sailed into the ports bringing with them much needed food supplies. They sold their precious cargo to both sides and made a killing. With their ill-gotten gains the fishermen were able to finance the building of houses in the style which had so impressed them on their trips to North Africa. Although Olhão is not a town to suit all tastes, it is without a doubt one of the region's most interesting.

SIGHTSEEING

Igreja Matriz de Nossa Senhora do Rosário

A 17th-century church with wonderful *talhas douradas* (gilt wood-carvings) and a typically Algarvian barrel-vaulted crypt (*abóbada de berço*). Annexed to the church is the small *Capela do Senhor Jesus dos Aflitos,* where the local fishing families light candles to appease the wind and the waves.

Market hall

✦ In the mornings, this picturesque market hall in the harbour is a real hive of activity.

Meat and vegetables are sold on the left hand side, while fish and shellfish are confined to the right. Senhor Henrique runs the barber shop opposite the market hall on the left, which doubles up as an art studio. He is always very happy to receive visitors. The *tascas* on the promenade serve good, cheap food.

Nossa Senhora da Soledade

This church took the local fishermen 17 years to build. It is crowned by a splendid Mosque-like dome that bears witness to the town's former prosperity. This is where the annual Easter procession starts.

Rua Capitão João Carlos Mendoça

A Trip to the Islands

(K 5-6) A favourite haunt for many Portuguese are the islands of Armona and Culatra. They are ideal for a day trip.

INFORMATION

Sailing times of ferry from Olhão

Peak season, Mon-Sat from Olhão to Armona 07.45-20.30 hrs, returning 07.00-20.45 hrs
Sun and public holidays 08.00-20.00 hrs, returning 08.30-20.30 hrs
Olhão to Culatra daily 07.10-19.30 hrs, returning 07.25-20.05 hrs

SURROUNDING AREA

Estói   (15)

Ten kilometres north-west of Olhão is Estói, best known for its diminutive ★ pink palace set in the middle of a wild and romantic garden. Its regal stairways, ornamental lakes, splashing fountains and azulejos painted with art nouveau motifs, are all unfor-

The castle of Estói was modelled on the classic Italian villa

tunately in a state of dilapidation. The town authorities bought the palace several years ago from the *Conde de Carvalhal*, and as soon as they have collected enough funds, restoration should get under way. If you soft-talk the gardener he'll allow you to walk through the garden to look at the marble statues. Archaeologists have unearthed a Roman site between the palace and Milreu. These excavations have also uncovered many bronze age pieces. At the Milreu exit on the road to Lisbon, you can see further evidence of Roman and Arabic occupation. This site includes the remains of mosaic baths built by a Roman nobleman. Between Estói and Moncarapacho is the *Restaurant Monte do Casal*. Set in expansive grounds, this well-tended country manor has 9 rooms and 5 suites.
Daily (except Mon); Tel 915 03; Category 1

Moncarapacho (K5)
This old Arab village, filled with sprawling greenhouses, is Portugal's biggest horticultural centre. The focal point of the village is the *Igreja Matriz* which has an impressive Renaissance portal. At the exit of the village is an interesting pottery (*closed Sat*) where the round Algarvian chimneys are still turned by hand. Practical objects as well as mythical figurines, half bird of prey/half lion, are also made here. Tucked away off the road to Santa Catarina, 2 km from Moncarapacho, is the *Hotel Adolfo da Quinta*. This delightful country hotel is set in a picturesque garden with a golf course. Evening meals are also available for non-residents.
80 rooms; Tel 792 519 (reservations necessary); Category 1

São Miguel & Cerro da Cabeça (K 5)
At 411 m, crowned with television and radio masts, *São Miguel* is the highest peak of the Serra de Monte Figo ★ ⬇. A spectacular view of the surrounding countryside and the ocean beyond can be seen from its summit. On the other side of the mountain lies the *Cerro da Cabeça*, a popular place for pot-holing. Most tourist offices have detailed maps of the area.

TAVIRA

(L5) ★ The eastern and western sides of this fascinating town are linked by a Roman bridge. The broad river that divides Tavira in two adopts a new name as it flows into the town through the seven archs of the ancient bridge. From its source, hundreds of kilometres up in the mountains, to the bridge the river is known as the *Séqua*. From the bridge to its estuary it becomes the *Rio Gilão*. The rise and fall of the town of Tavira is closely linked to the course of this river. Long ago, galleons, caravels and trading ships sailed up and down its waters and weighed anchor in the harbour. After the earthquake of 1755, however, the river silted up and became inaccessible to all maritime traffic, except for small fishing boats. Since then the old Moorish capital has fallen into a kind of fairy-tale slumber. Inhabited by just 8000 people, it still has the air of a sleepy time-forgotten town. The river banks are lined with elegant, patrician houses, whose splendid architecture is a reminder of the town's former prosperity. Equally elegant are the 34 churches, chapels and monasteries. The Gilão still plays an important role in the religious community, as it is used for baptisms, and once a year there is a ceremony in which the river itself is blessed.

For those with an eye for architecture, Tavira has a fascinating mixture of decorative styles: Renaissance windows, latticed wooden doors, elaborate balconies, Oriental roofs. Many of these fine architectural features are very well preserved. Under Arab rule, Balsa, as the town was then called, was an important centre of Moorish culture. Many artists, poets and musicians lived, worked, and often performed here. But in 1242 the town was conquered by Dom Paio Peres Correia, and the Arab court was banished. To understand the town and capture its true charm, it is best explored on foot: wander through its narrow alleys and down its steps; look inside its churches; visit the castle ruins and admire the windows that grace the old Arab strongholds; and stand before the portal of the *Igreja da Misericórdia,* a jewel of the Renaissance.

For a touch of greenery, wander through the park and continue along the road lined with palm trees, past the salt marshes, and down to the docks. There is a regular ferry service that goes from here to the *Ilha de Tavira,* which has a good beach frequented by locals, as well as a camp-site. These wide open spaces make a refreshing change from the rocky landscape that characterizes most of the rest of the Algarve's coast.

SIGHTSEEING

Castelo

All that remains of the ancient castle are its thick boundary walls, but they enclose an enchanting little garden. A set of well worn steps leads up to a view over the unique roof-tops of Tavira. On summer evenings groups of musicians and choirs often stage performances here.
Calçada Dom Paio Peres Correia

Churches

Igreja da Misericórdia was one of the few churches to survive the earthquake in relatively good condition. It has the most impressive Renaissance portal in the

---

The cursed lovers

If you happen to be in Tavira on 24 June for the festival of São João, stop by the Vaz Varela fountain. Stick around and you might catch a glimpse of the two young Moorish lovers who have been waiting to fall into each others arms for years. According to legend they were turned to stone as they were about to embrace and are still waiting to be freed from this terrible curse. This apparation, however, can only be seen between midnight and sunrise.

Algarve, which is surmounted with the town's coat of arms and a royal crown. Inside are a Rococo altar, some fine gilt wood carvings (*talhas douradas*) and azulejos. *Travessa da Fonte*

Igreja do Carmo was once part of the old Carmelite Convent. It houses some important examples of 18th-century gilt wood carvings, particularly those that decorate the choir stalls. At the back of the church there is a small forgotten graveyard, with gravestones dating back to the middle ages. *Largo do Carmo*

Igreja Santa Maria do Castelo is Tavira's main church. It was built in 1244 on the site of a mosque, but all that remains of the original structure is a Gothic portal. Seven holy knights, who were allegedly murdered by Moors in the 13th century, are said to be buried in front of the altar. Whether true or false, the story provided the justification needed for the barbaric act of revenge by Dom Paio Peres Correia, who drove the Moors out after a bloody battle. Thirty-three years later he too was buried here. The arabesque window of the bell tower serves as a reminder of the civilization he was determined to suppress. *Calçada Dom Paio Peres Correia*

The *Igreja São Paulo* features some beautiful azulejos and 17th century gilt wood carvings. Paintings from the Flemish school hang above the 16th century altar of the *Capela Nossa Senhora de Consulação, Praça 5 de Outubro*

MUSEUM

Arquivo Histórico
A few years ago, a group of students, led by a professor at the Algarve University, undertook the reorganization of the town's municipal library collections and its historic archives. These are both now stored in the Casa Cabria, a historic building opposite the eastern side of the Roman bridge. The collection includes some rare 16th century documents.

RESTAURANTS

Beira Rio
◁▷ Offers a splendid evening view of the Roman bridge and the old houses on the opposite bank of the Rio Gilão.
Borda Agua Asseca 48 (left after the bridge and through the old archway); Category 2

Imperial
◁▷ A pleasant place to eat on warm summer evenings. The tables are arranged on the pavement outside with a view over

The whitewashed houses of the ancient Moorish capital, Tavira

the river and grand houses on the opposite bank. The *arroz de marisco* (seafood risotto) is particularly good.
Rua José Padinha 22 (river promenade); Category 2-3

HOTELS

Eurotel
This hotel is on the N 125, roughly 2 km out of town. Bungalows are also available for rent. Swimming pool, tennis courts and a garden.
80 rooms; Quinta das Oliveiras; Tel: 588 530, Fax: 513 072; Category 2

Pension Lagoas
A little old-fashioned, but comfortable and neat.
16 rooms; Rua Almirante Cândido dos Reis 24 (east town); Tel: 222 52, Category 3

Quinta do Caracol
★ This is one of the *casas de habitaçãos* – traditonal houses, usually old manor houses, where guests are treated like one of the family. This particular *quinta* has been converted into seven private apartments, and is set in a beautiful garden that's full of delightful features.
São Pedro (1st exit after Tavira coming from Faro); Tel: 224 75, Fax: 231 75; Category 2

Residencial Princesa do Gilão
Well-appointed hotel in the centre of town on the east bank.
23 rooms with en-suite bathroom; Rua Borda de Agua de Aguiar 10-12; Tel and Fax: 325 5171; Category 2

SPORT & LEISURE

Swimming
For a day out on the beach, you can hop on a ferry from the jetty at the end of the river promenade that will take you across to the Ilha de Tavira.
Daily (peak season) 07.55-20.30 hrs

Bike hire
Rua Dr Parreira 135, next to the Restaurant O Caneção; Tel: 81282

INFORMATION

Posto de Turismo
Daily 09.30-20.00 hrs; Praça da República; Tel: 225 11

SURROUNDING AREA

Fonte Salgada (L5)
About 3 km north of Tavira, set amid some breathtaking scenery, is this forgotten little village. There is a small waterfall nearby.
Moinhos da Rocha

Luz de Tavira (K5)
West of Tavira, 6 km along the road to Faro, is this satellite vil-

lage. Its skyline is dominated by a 16th-century church, an example of Portuguese Manueline architecture at its finest. The portal is richly decorated and the interior is tiled with arabesque azulejos. About 2 km south-east of the village, along the road that leads to the graveyard, stand the ruins of *Torre de Aires* and *Balsa,* an ancient Roman settlement. A great place to enjoy the view and spectacular sunsets.

Ria Formosa   (K–L5)

There is a lovely path that starts from Tavira and runs parallel to Ria Formosa. This long line of lagoons stretches for 50 km from Cacela Velha to Faro and is protected from the sea by large sandbanks. Ninety per cent of Portugal's oysters and shellfish are fished from these muddy waters. The *Parque Natural da Ria Formosa* (*Rua Teófilo Braga 15, Faro; Tel: 704 134*) is an immense nature reserve covering 18 400 hectares between Faro and Vila Real de Santo António. It is a resting place for migratory birds en route to Africa, and the nesting ground for wading birds such as herons and storks, which forage by the river banks, as well as terns, gannets and the occasional kingfisher. A wide variety of fish, crustaceans, chameleons and lizards also thrive in this protected area. If you want to get a closer look at the wading birds and marine life, you will have to be prepared to walk a fair distance, and keep your eyes constantly peeled.

Beaches   (K–L5)

The best beaches are to be found on the various sand islands bordering the lagoon, which are not as crowded as the beaches around Olhão. 6 km east of Tavira, the resort of Cabana/Conceição, once a picturesque fishing village, has suffered at the hands of the developers and is now overrun with blocks of holiday apartments. Every other building is either a restaurant, café, or bar, but you can escape the tourist hustle and bustle by taking a trip to the long sandy beaches of the lagoon. Bask in the sun among brightly coloured fishing boats. Wander around the grounds of the 19th-century Fort João de Barra. The interior is not open to the public, but the moat, defensive walls and emblazoned portal are worth a look. The beach directly in front of the fort is ideal for children. *Santa Luzia,* a quiet fishing village that lies on the Ria Formosa, is a 45-minute walk from Tavira along the palm-lined river bank. Directly opposite the boat moorings is an idiosyncratic restaurant called the *Oceano* (*Wed–Sun 19.00-24.00 hrs; Category 3*) run by a Swedish woman, Anna, and her Portuguese colleague. Together they concoct delicious vegetarian dishes, and run a well-stocked bar, making it a perfect place to enjoy a sundowner. A little further on, the *Marisqueira Capelo* (*Daily except Wed; Category 2-3*) serves more traditional Portuguese cuisine. Here you can dine alfresco while watching the sun go down.

VILA REAL DE SANTO ANTONIO

(**M4**) This small town (pop. 13 000) with its pretty harbour is situated on the Rio Guadiana that marks the frontier between Spain and Portugal. The symmetrical streets are lined with rows of shops, and there are many buildings of architectural interest. The streets were laid out on a grid plan put together by the Marquês de Pombal in 1774. He was very keen to follow the latest town planning trends, to endorse Portugal's affluence, and impress its great neighbouring nation.

Centuries ago most of the trade in the area revolved around the nearby Spanish harbour of Ayamonte. Then, in the Middle Ages, two fishing villages on the Portuguese side of the river developed into trade centres: Monte Gordo and Santo António de Arenilha challenged the commercial supremacy of their neighbour. The sea, however, proved too wild, and every year the waves claimed back more land. Santo António de Arenilha was eventually completely engulfed by a tidal wave. Monte Gordo was luckier and managed to escape the rising waters, and by the 18th century it had developed into a settlement inhabited by 5000 fishermen and their families. During this period, the ambitious and confident Marquis of Pombal decided to recreate a new Portuguese harbour town on the Guadiana border to replace the one that had been destroyed by the sea. Houses were built in Lisbon and transported ready assembled to the site of the new harbour. In less than six months they had been erected along the regular network of streets. But somehow the town of Vila Real never took root. Nobody wanted to live in these houses and they remained uninhabited. Though ad-

mired by the leading lights as a perfect example of the latest in town planning, the necessary spark of life never entered its ordered structure. Neither did its pompous name (literally 'the Royal City of Santo António', in memory of the submerged village) help to give it life and soul.

Until recently, a ferry pulled into the harbour every 20 minutes, and the town was a hive of activity, with a seasonal influx of 13 000 tourists crossing its border. The recently completed bridge across the Rio Guadiana, 4 km north of the town, however, now carries the burden of traffic that once congested the town. The Spain-Portugal road bypasses Vila Real, transporting holidaymakers direct to the beaches. The original architecture, however, makes Vila Real de Santo António an interesting port of call.

RESTAURANTS

D. Jotta
The menu offers both regional specialities and international cuisine and the restaurant itself boasts a lovely view of the Guadiana estuary.
Ponta de Piedade; Tel 43151; Category 2

Edmundo
In this simple restaurant, salads and fish dishes are the speciality. Predominantly Spanish clientele.
Avenida da República 55; Tel: 446 89; Category 3

HOTEL

Hotel Guadiana
General Franco once held talks with Salazar in this hotel, which

The black and white mosaic paving of the Praça Marquês de Pombal in Vila Real

is almost a national monument. You can see Spain from its windows. Facilities for the disabled. *37 rooms; Avenida da República 94; Tel: 511 482/92, Fax: 511 478; Category 2*

INFORMATION

Posto de Turismo
Daily 09.00-19.00 hrs; Praça Marquês de Pombal (opposite the ferry port); Tel: 432 72

SURROUNDING AREA

Cacela Velha   (L5)
★ ⚜ Romantic village that lies 16 km west of Vila Real on the edge of the lagoon, with a sandbank that is ideal for swimming and sunbathing. It is a small settlement with a 12th century fort, which today houses the coastguard station. The large church dominates the village, but is nothing special. The only restaurant in town, on the other hand, is definitely worth a visit for those who like fresh fish.

Manta Rota   (L5)
The population of this fishing village, 14 km west of Vila Real, trebles during the busy season. Its broad flat beach, which is particularly suitable for children, makes it a popular resort with Potuguese families. There are various watersport facilities available and a number of beach huts that can be hired for the summer. The first kiosk on the right on the way down to the beach rents out mopeds and bicycles. The *Estalagem Oásis* is a remarkably friendly small hotel close to the beach with facilities for the disabled. *20 rooms; Praia da Lota; Tel: 951 644, Fax: 951 660; Category 1-2*

Excursions on the Guadiana (M 3-4)
★ ⚜ The Rio Guadiana is a wide river that forms a natural border between Spain and Portugal. It is navigable from the ancient Roman garrison of Mértola in Alentejo right down to its estuary at Vila Real da Santo António. A good way of exploring the river beyond the harbour is to go on one of the organized motor boat excursions; a very pleasant and relaxing way to spend the day. You can enjoy the absolute calm of the unspoilt landscape on both sides of the Guadiana, and observe the many different bird species that nest along its banks. The boats depart from the marina in Vila Real (100 m left of the pier) and the day trips run on Tuesdays, Wednesdays and Sundays. It costs 6,000 Esc. per person; children under 10 go half price. The fee includes a typical Algarve lunch, served when the boat stops in one of the villages further up the river. *(Tel: 440 77)*

The California of Europe

*The reputation of the Algarve was built on its beaches,
coves and luxury hotel complexes*

The beaches most coveted by tourists in the Algarve lie to the west of Faro. All of them are fine and sandy, but their settings vary greatly: some are flat and seemingly endless, with the occasional dune on the horizon; some are small, bordered by steeply rising red cliffs; others lie tucked away in the crevices of bizarre rock formations. And then, of course, there are the beaches set against the less natural backdrop of apartment blocks, hotels and holiday villas. In summer, the majority of these beaches are overflowing with tourists. There are still a few, however, which do not get so crowded, where there's more room to breathe and relax. These are, of course, the less accessible beaches that can only be reached by boat (many of the local fishermen are happy to act as ferrymen) or after a lengthy walk.

Just thirty years ago Albufeira was a tranquil place where the Portuguese came to get away from it all. Today the secret is out and the town has been caught in the wave of tourism

ALBUFEIRA

(E5, G5) Once upon a time, Albufeira, with its narrow streets, charmingly crooked houses and a beautiful old town gate, was just a sleepy seaside village. The locals played billiards in the artist Bailote's bar, where their *bica* was served on wobbly marble-topped tables, and where on cold winter nights they warmed themselves with a glass of *medronho*. In the harbour, the men darned their fishing nets, and painted colourful eyes on their boats, to ward off the evil eye. Every day, a man on a tractor would wait on the beach to haul in the boats as they returned with their catch. He was a retired engineer, who liked to lend a helping hand to these hardworking fishermen. In the summer, a handful of foreigners met here. Twenty-five years ago you wouldn't have seen more than a handful of foreigners wandering along the beaches of this idyllic place. These early tourists loved this village, its people, and its sleepy, friendly atmosphere. Then, slowly, they started to bring friends with them, who

MARCO POLO SELECTION: BARLAVENTO

1 Crazy Golf
Fun for all the family at this 18-hole mini-golf course, complete with pizzeria, restaurant, billiards and pool (page 54)

2 São Lourenço dos Matos
One of the most sumptuous churches in Portugal, lined with gold and azulejos (page 57)

3 Centro Cultural São Lourenço
A gallery in a unique architectural setting. Exhibitions, concerts, conferences, and readings all take place regularly here (page 57)

4 Marina de Vilamoura
Ships, boats and yachts of every description and nationality moor in this cosmopolitan marina (page 60)

then brought their friends. All fell under the spell of Albufeira. It was a town where people could happily imagine growing old. The word spread and Albufeira's transformation began.

Today's visitor may find this fairy-tale picture of Albufeira hard to imagine. The quiet village of yester-year has become a model of the modern holiday resort, in which tourism has altered the people as much as it has altered the town's streets. Back in the days when the village was still sleepy, there was only one shopping street, and no one would have dreamed of wearing shorts while walking through the town (the Portuguese share with the Islamic cultures of Africa and the Middle East the custom of modest dress). Surprisingly, despite its numerous face-lifts and redevelopment, waves of newly converted tourists still flood in to Albufeira every year, and the crowd it is drawing in is an increasingly young one. So, if you want to meet people and party, then this is the place to dance the night away, the Algarve's most 'happening' resort.

The town council has attempted to restrict the effects of the building boom. Multi-storey apartment blocks are thankfully absent from the town centre as well as the sea front. Most of the new houses are confined to the steep mountainsides, and much of the town centre has been pedestrianized. There is no disputing the fact that the surrounding beaches are wonderful. Most can be reached by car via a newly completed tunnel bored through the cliff-face. You can also get to them by boat from the old fishing harbour: just come out of the port, turn left and head east.

To get a feel for what this old fishing village must once have been like, take a stroll through the old town centre at the heart of which stands a monument to Albufeira's most famous inhabitant, Vicente de Santo António, a 17th-century Augustinian monk and missionary, who died in Nagasaki. Albufeira's history goes back 2000 years. Under the Romans it was called Baltum, but the Moors changed this to Albhuar, which means 'the castle by the sea'. Because of its location on a cliff overlooking the Atlantic, the town was virtually impregnable. The earthquakes and floods of 1755, however, swallowed up the lower town. In 1893, during the Portuguese Civil War, the town suffered further damage, when monarchist soldiers besieged and set light to it, killing many of their Liberal enemies. Small wonder then, that few historical sites remain. The hospital and the old town hall, with its filigree bell tower, now stand where the castle once stood. Compare these buildings with the new town hall on the eastern edge of the town, and you will quickly realize how much Albufeira has changed with the times.

RESTAURANTS

Cabaz da Praia/Beachbasket

A well-established restaurant with a French owner, and a charming flower-filled terrace. Good, unconventional cooking.
Praça Miguel Bombarda; Category 1-2

O Dias

A cupboard-sized eatery with a sea-view terrace, and good solid charcoal-grilled dishes.
Praça Miguel Bombarda; Category 3

Evaristo

A well-hidden restaurant nestling in the cliffs of the Praia do Castelo, with a terrace overlooking the beach. It is renowned for its fish dishes. Go through the archway inscribed Quinta do Castelo, and carry straight down to the beach. In summer, reservations are a must.
Tel: 591 666; Category 1

Paraiso

Brazilian *churrasqueira* with great steaks and other specialities from the grill. Enjoy a pilsner beer or a range of Portuguese wines with your meal. The restaurant boasts a tropical garden with a waterfall, alcoves with flowering plants, and romantic seating under shady trees. Frequent live bands.
Areias de São João/Praia da Oura; Tel: 513 303; Category 2

A Ruina

This establishment behind the old fish market has always specialized in seafood. Diners eat at long wooden tables.
Tel: 512094; Category 1-2

Três Coroas

Dine beneath the trees on the patio. Occasionally proceedings are accompanied by fado musicians.
Rua do Correio Velho 8; Tel: 512 640; Category 2

SHOPPING

High quality ceramic goods can be found at *Infante Dom Henrique (Rua Cândido dos Reis 30)*. Fine pewter ware and Vista Alegre porcelain can be found at *Bobi*, just left of the fishing harbour. *Abrakadabra,* in the pedestrian zone, has an unusual selection of jewellery. South American ornaments and jewellery can be found at *Apumanke*, at the top of the steps on the right, immediately before the cliff tunnel.
Rua 5 de Outobro 3

HOTELS

California

A pretty, old-town hotel with roof-top garden and pool.

56 rooms, Rua Cândido dos Reis; Tel: 586 833, Fax: 586 850; Category 1-2

Sheraton Algarve

This impressive hotel complex, with its dancing fountains and extensive grounds, resembles a stately home. The hotel offers individually decorated rooms, some of which are designated for non-smokers. It also has good sport and fitness facilities, all situated amidst some of the most spectacular coastal scenery in the Algarve. 8 km from Albufeira.

203 rooms, 12 suites; Praia da Falésia; Tel: 501 999, Fax: 501 950; Category L

Vila Galé Praia

A four-star hotel by the beach, with private pool and tennis courts.

40 rooms; Praia do Galé; Tel: 591 050, Fax: 591 436; Category 1-2

Vila Joya

This small hotel in a converted villa lies 6 km west of Albufeira on Galé beach. The rooms are all exquisitely decorated. Restaurant predominantly French.

16 rooms; Restaurant reservations, Tel: 591 795; Category L

SPORT & LEISURE

A wide range of watersport facilities are available including waterskiing and surfing. The best surf is at Galé beach, west of Albufeira. The best snorkelling is between Albufeira and the Praia do Castelo, or just before the Praia da Oura, to the east of Albufeira. The closest golf courses are in Vilamoura, with riding at Estalagem da Cegonha in Vilamoura.

★ Crazy Golf: An entertaining day out with the family can be spent at Lagoa de Viseu near Algoz, about 15 minutes from the coast. An 18-hole mini-golf course with entertaining obstacles is complemented by a children's animal park, where the animals can be stroked, and pony rides. There's also a pool, bar and pizzeria. To get there, turn off the N125 at Guia, in the direction of Algoz, and follow the signs. Daily from 10.00 hrs; children 550$00, adults 750$00; Tel: 54134

You can go on small excursions by fishing boat to the local grottoes. The Gruta do Xorino, near the Praia de Baleeira, was once used as a refuge for Liberals fleeing Albufeira in the face of the monarchist onslaught of the town in 1833. They escaped to the cave by means of an underground passage, where they were picked up by a boat that transported them to the relative safety of Faro. Today, people still claim that this grotto has special magic powers.

ENTERTAINMENT

The Kadoc is a hi-tech, up-market club with several dance floors, a tropical night-club and a champagne bar. This happening spot, which lies on the old road between Albufeira and the Vilamoura turn-off should not be missed. It is no longer ranked, however, as the region's biggest disco: the H_2O in the mock catacombs of the Aquashow on the road to Quartiera is a megadisco that is more comparable with the kind of venue found in Ibiza. Discos around here rarely open before 23.00 hrs, and they don't start to hot up until after midnight, but they stay open all night and you can dance until dawn.

The *Kiss* Club plays easy-going dance music, and attracts a 'not-so-young' clientele.

Opposite the Hotel Aldeia, *Liberto's Disco-Bar* does a brisk trade at around 6 pm when people flock here to enjoy a sundowner. The canny DJ targets a range of audiences, with 1940s and 1950s music on Mondays, 1960s sounds on Wednesdays, and Rock'n'Roll on Fridays. Prices are those of a normal bar. *3km east of Albufeira in Areias de São João*

Locomia, in *Praia de Santa Eulalia,* is chic and elegant, but not uncomfortably so. Offering good food and hot rhythms, it counts amongst the best discotheques in the area, with a price to match. *(Restaurant Tel: 513 636)*

For years now, *Michel's* in *Montechoro* has been one of the region's top night-clubs of the more traditional sort, with good floor shows, decent cooking, and entertainment for the whole family. *(Tel: 515 997)*

Portuguese and foreigners meet and mix perfectly in ✝ *Splash (Areias de São João).* Young clientele.

The ✝ *Summertime Club (Vila Magna, Montechoro),* is another favourite with steadfast nocturnals. The most adept of DJs plays a set perfectly adapted to the changing mood of the young, party-hungry crowd.

INFORMATION

Posto de Tourismo
Daily 09.00 - 19.00 hrs; Rua 5 de Outubro; Tel: 512 144/525 428

SURROUNDING AREA

Armação de Pêra (D-E5/G5)
The town itself is swamped in apartment blocks and high-rise hotels. Thankfully the beach, which lies well to the east, is relatively unspoilt and only the distant skyline reminds you of the damage wrought by tourism. The sea remains shallow for hundreds of metres and is ideal for paddling and wallowing in the water. Between this beach and Galé beach there is an area set aside for nude bathing.

The *Vila Vita Parc* which lies on the sea front in Porches, between Armação and Carvoeiro, is a luxury complex with hotel, apartments and restaurants in a tropical park. It features palm groves, water falls, in-and-outdoor pools, and a range of sports facilities. Next door is a new golf course with helpful staff. Over the top luxury, Hollywood style. *194 rooms; Alporchinchos/Armação de Pêra; Tel: 315 310, Fax 315 333; Category L.* In the same complex, but independently run, is the *Vila Vita Vital-Center,* a health centre specialising in diagnosis, therapy and rehabilitation. Many treatments are offered: Chinese medicine, homoeopathy, chiropractic therapy, etc. *Tel: 310 112*

The 18th-century castle in the town of Armação de Pêra has one of the finest views in the area. To the east lies the *Praia Dourada,* the safest stretch of beach on the Algarve coast, while to the west the bizarre rock formations and caves which can only be reached by boat can be seen. Between these promontories you can glimpse the smaller bathing bays and their beaches: *Praia dos*

Nossa Senhora da Rocha — small chapel in an idyllic setting

Beijinhos (Beach of Kisses), the *Praia dos Irmãos* (The Brother's Beach), and *Maré Grande* (The Beach of the Great Flood).

Nossa Senhora da Rocha   (D5)

The scenery along the coast road from Armação de Pêra to Nossa Senhora da Rocha (about 1.5 km) will provide a welcome relief after the overdeveloped resorts you have left behind. Here, a rock plateau rises to meet the ocean, and the sheer cliff face plunges 30 m to the sea below. Right on the apex of the cliff stands the diminutive 🌿 chapel of Our Blessed Lady of the Rocks, *Nossa Senhora da Rocha*.

It's easy to lose yourself in the beauty of this place, where the rush and chaos of daily life seems far away. In August the parish bishop celebrates a ==mass for the fishermen and their boats.== Standing on the plateau, he casts down his blessing on the boats, which are specially decorated from top to bottom with flags, flowers and bunting. They make a picturesque sight, lined up as if for a parade, bobbing merrily in the water. On both sides of the cliff are beaches which are connected to one another by a tunnel. The unique atmosphere is only slightly tainted by the big hotel complex which lies to the west.

Olhos de Água   (E5/H5)

This small, attractive beach lies 7 km east of Albufeira, and is much frequented throughout the summer. Fresh water springs shoot up from the seabed, making swirling patterns on the surface. Hence the name Olhos de Água, meaning 'eyes of water'.

Praia da Falésia   (E5/H5)

Here, the beach rolls gently for miles, the sea is similarly shallow, and there is space to relax and play. It's a child's paradise. The beach is protected from the strong north winds by a 30 m-high, red cliff face which towers over it. The powerful contrast between the colourful cliff and the miles of pale flatland makes the scenery particularly striking. On top of the cliff is a pine forest.

ALMANSIL

(F5/H5) Although just a one-street town, that is increasingly inhabited by the English, who run the majority of shops, restaurants, and bars, the village of Almansil is also the gateway to many of Barlavento's finest beaches and holiday resorts. The nearer you get to Vale de Lobo the more exclusive (and interesting) the shops become. Borboleta is worth a visit for its quality crystal shop. (*On the Quarteira road*)

RESTAURANTS

Pequeno Mundo
A big country house with many rooms, restaurant and a pleasant atmosphere. Reservations a must.
Closed Mondays; Pereiras/Almansil; Tel: 399 866; Category L-1

Pig and Whistle
English local, serving cheap and cheerful pub grub with a menu for vegetarians. Particularly suitable for families with children, who will be given their own table and menu. There are specially provided table mats which they can colour in while they wait. A meal out on the patio is particularly recommended in summer.
Daily (except Sat and Sun), children's hour 18.45-19.45 hrs; N 125; Tel: 395 216; Category 2

Smoky Joe's
Restaurant with an old domed ceiling and Mexican food.
Evenings only; Rua 5 de Outubro 85; Tel: 393 077; Category 2

O Tradicional
A simple, down-to-earth restaurant, in accordance with current trend. Good Portuguese-French cuisine and fine service.
Closed Sundays; Estrada do Vale do Lobo; Tel: 399 093; Category 1

SHOPPING

Almansil is a good place for shopping. There are some good shops for interior furnishings and a great supermarket (*Apolónia*) with a wide choice of international products. The *Griffin Bookshop* stocks books in five languages. *All in Rua 5 Outubro.*

SURROUNDING AREA

Capela de São Lourenço dos Matos   (I 5)
★ This jewel of a church lies just 3 km from the town, on the way to Faro. Inside, it is decorated with blue and white azulejos which were made by Policarpo de Oliveira Bernardes in the 1730s. They depict the story of St Lawrence from his birth in the 3rd century, in the Spanish kingdom of Aragon, to his eventual martyrdom. This small church is one of the finest in all Portugal. Entrance is of course free, but there is a donation box, and all contributions for the purchase of a new organ are gratefully received.

Centro Cultural   (I 5)
★ The collection of small houses huddled around São Lourenço's church have been converted into a cultural centre and gallery where Portuguese and international artists are exhibited. The centre plays host to classical, avant-garde, jazz and rock musicians, as well as traditional Portuguese fado singers. Poets and

novelists also give readings, and the painting summer school welcomes participants from all over the globe. Performances are often followed by discussion groups, and the curators are known to offer their guests a glass or two of wine. In 1996 the centre celebrated its 15th anniversary. If you cross the Faro-Portimão motorway and take the footpath through the fields you'll come to the *Quinta da Calma*, a spiritualist centre which offers unique holidays. *(Tel: 393 741, Fax: 393346)*

Quinta do Lago/ Vale do Lobo (F 5/H 5)

This luxury holiday complex has endless beaches and dunes, and doesn't even get over-crowded in the summer. This is because it's a little more out of the way than most other holiday resorts. It's an extension of the Ilha de Faro, and can be reached via an old wooden bridge which spans the lagoon. The water here is well stocked with fish and shellfish and, coming over the dunes, the view of the Atlantic stretches to the horizon. The beach runs for miles in both directions, an ideal place for a relaxing walk by the sea. Or else venture inland and explore the deserted dunes, where you won't see a soul for miles.

Quinta do Lago is among the finest holiday complexes in Portugal. Accommodation comes in the form of spacious villas and apartments, and a choice of luxury hotels, all set in a pine forest. Everything is of the highest quality, and golfers are especially well catered for. There are four interconnecting courses which lie between Quinta do Lago and the luxury resort of Vale do Lobo.

Vale do Lobo is a more densely populated holiday resort, with the emphasis firmly on sport: once again, golfers are given priority and the resort's course claims to have the most spectacular hole in Portugal. To reach the green from the fairway, you have to drive over a sheer cliff-face which drops down to the beach below. The resort is a particular favourite among English tourists.

Restaurants in the area tend towards the expensive. The *Casa de Torre Hermitage,* though owned by a Dutchman, serves French cuisine in a pleasant country house atmosphere *(Daily except Mon; Estrada de Vale do Lobo; Tel: 394 329; Category L)*. The *São Gabriel* is renowned for its fine cooking and is particularly welcoming of children. *(Daily except Mon; On the street between Vale do Lobo and Quinta do Lago; Tel: 394 521; Category 1)*

A special feature of the area are the beach restaurants, which line the shore between the two resorts. The jet set meet at *João Passos* on the Ancão beach, where João and his Dutch wife have been setting the trends for years. Look down on the beach from the spacious terrace and enjoy the fine seafood in the company of the in-crowd *(Praia do Ancão; Category 1-2)*. Making sure that João doesn't get all the action, the *Tropical Restaurant* which is right next door draws an equally well-heeled crowd. Decorated with exotic plants, the ambience is... well, tropical. The speciality is lobster. Reservation for dinner is a must. *(Tel: 398123; Category 1)*

In the old days, ❀ *Julia's Bar* was run by its eponymous Angolan proprietor, who was a

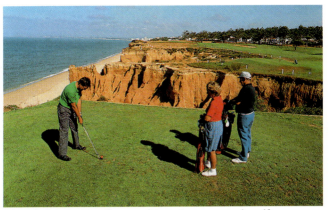

The Vale do Lobo. Tee off on one of Europe's most spectacular golf courses

legendary figure on the local scene. She ran the restaurant at the top of the cliff, and the beach beneath it bears her name. The view is as spectacular as ever, but now the bar's owners are English and, if not as legendary, continue to serve good food and drink in a beautiful setting. *(Praia da Júlia; Category 2)*

Quinta do Lago is not only the name of the town, but also its finest hotel: sea views, Japanese-style gardens, pools, a health club and fine restaurants *(132 rooms; Tel: 396 666, Fax: 396 393; Category L)*. The counterpart of this in Vale do Lobo is the *Dona Filipa*. Among the finest establishments in the Algarve, it is originally decorated and stands right at the sea's edge. The food, however, is not as refined as the prices might lead you to expect. *(141 rooms; Tel: 394 141; Category L)*

The area is ideal for people who love nothing more than sea, sun and golf – or any number of other sports. The range of sporting facilities on offer is enormous. The *Barrington Club* in Vale do Lobo runs a golf school, and has tennis, squash, snooker, gymnastics and table tennis facilities. The social scene is also lively. An excellent masseur practises here. He was originally stationed in Alentejo as a pilot, until he met the love of his life who brought him to Barlavento where he now works. *(Reservations Tel 396622)*

If it's night-life you're looking for, the *Kasbah Nightclub* in Vale do Lobo is where the young and beautiful hang out. Dancing, live music and drinking until the early hours *(21.30-04.00 hrs)*, with all sorts of dance music, and special guest appearances from prominent Portuguese musicians.

Three of the finest golf courses in the area are to be found in Quinta do Lago *(Tel: 394 529)*, graded according to ability: both the beginner and the professional are catered for. Reservations for the *Vale do Lobo Golf Club, Tel: 394 444*. *Mini-golf* can be played opposite the Hotel Dona Filipa in Vale do Lobo, but it is rather expensive: around £5 per child. Adults naturally pay more.

For tours of the beach and surrounding area on horseback: *Horse's Riding Paradise* (*between Almansil and Quinta do Lago*; *Tel: 396468*)

Tennis courts are plentiful. Britain's own David Lloyd has a centre here with four sand and eight clay courts. (*Tel: 393 939*)

Watersports facilities are available on all beaches. Surfboards can be hired on the *Vale do Lobo beach*, on the far side of the resort. Carrying on further east, you'll pass a row of beach huts which line the long stretch of sand leading to *Quinta do Lago*. In this elegant holiday resort, you'll need to dress smartly, especially around the *Bougainvillea Plaza,* where the well-groomed and well-heeled hang out. The Moroccan style disco *Trigonometria* is a popular night spot, while the chic *Montinho* has a French flair, and has always attracted the in-crowd from Lisbon.

VILAMOURA

(**F5/H5**) Between the sprawl of concrete hotels and apartments which define the Algarve's less attractive side, and the infinitely preferable ambience of Albufeira, stands the enormous holiday resort of Vilamoura. Holiday villages, golf courses and an ultra-modern marina with room for yachts, catamarans, and dinghies, as well as fishing boats, characterize the area. Vilamoura is well-planned, a direct response to the chaotic high-rise building found further up the coast. Landlubbers and sea-dogs find equal respite in its well laid-out streets. If you've an interest in archaeology, there is even a Roman site at Cerro da

Vila, which is probably the only old thing you'll see in the whole town.

SIGHTSEEING

Cerro da Vila
This is the above-mentioned excavation site and lies to the west of the marina. As the archaeologists are still working on the site, viewing opportunities are limited.

Marina de Vilamoura
❧ Flags from all over the world flutter on the masts of every type of sailing vessel in this international marina: three-masted schooners, million dollar luxury yachts, Chinese junks, even an old paddle-steamer (which, incidentally, holds a restaurant) can be seen moored here.

RESTAURANTS

Lots to choose from, but none of them cheap. The round beach pavilion of the *Atlantis Hotel* is a comfortable place to eat. House speciality: *arroz de marisco,* Angolan-style risotto. *Praia de Marinha; Category 1-2*

HOTELS

Ampalius
❧ The design of this four-star hotel is circular and each room has a large balcony overlooking the sea. Children are well catered for. Facilities for the disabled. *357 rooms*; *Tel: 380 910, Fax: 380 911; Category 1-2*

Dom Pedro's
Hotel with many sporting facilities. Golf, tennis, pools, and a

conference centre. An efficient, high quality hotel. 43 of the 373 rooms are suites.
Tel: 389 650, Fax: 315482 (Dom Pedro Golf); Tel: 389 802, Fax: 313270 (Dom Pedro Marina); Category 1-2

Marinotel

A luxury hotel whose playful post-modern architecture mimics the design of a cruise liner. Standing between the marina and the Atlantic, it has a view unmatched in the vicinity. 369 rooms, of which 21 are suites; restaurants, pools, a health club and tennis courts complete the QE2 atmosphere. Art exhibitions are often held in the lobby.
Marina de Vilamoura; Tel: 389 988, Fax: 389 869, Category L

Vilamoura is also well supplied with self-catering apartments. Ask your travel agent for further information.

SPORT & LEISURE

Angling

A fishing licence is not obligatory. Scuba fishing is permitted only with a harpoon.

Beaches

Falésia: this beach stretches westwards from Vilamoura for miles. It is protected from the wind by the spectacular sandstone cliffs to the north. Surfers and windsurfers stay closer to Vilamoura where, because it is more exposed, the winds are more favourable.
Praia da Marinha: perfectly suited to children, as the sea here is calm. Directly behind the Hotel Atlantis.

Casino

As well as the usual gaming tables, this casino offers a wide range of gambling machines, restaurants, floor shows, and performances by its own resident dance troupe.

Clubs

Squash, snooker, tennis, badminton, bowling and aerobics in the *Rock Garden Sports and Leisure Centre. Tel: 314 740.*

Deep Sea Fishing

The *Big Game Fishing Centre* offers day-long trips in 14 m aluminium fishing boats.
Day excursions from 09.00-16.30 hrs; Marina de Vilamoura; Tel: 325 866

Golf

Vilamoura I: an 18-hole course with a beautiful green, which many consider to be difficult because the fairways go through a pine forest. (*Tel: 313 652*)
Vilamoura II (Dom Pedro): an easier course, though not as charming. (*Tel: 315 582*)
Vilamoura III: a new 9 + 9 + 9-hole course, which makes up for what it lacks in terms of landscape with an impressive clubhouse. (*Tel: 312 321*)

Riding

All the stables in the region keep reliable horses, and many have experienced instructors. Sunset rides, cliff-top rambles and jumping are all on offer.
Centro Hípico de Vilamoura: in the old *Estalagem da Cegonha,* this well-kept stable has an excellent indoor dressage hall and jumping arena. *Just outside the Vilamoura complex, on the way to Albufeira; Tel: 313 033.*

Rural beauty and steadfast tradition

Lively local customs amid the evergreen mountain landscape provide an interesting contrast to the coastal region

Characterized by the evergreen Monchique landscape, the Algarvian back country provides an interesting contrast to the more developed coastal regions. Folklore and tradition, mostly in the form of song and dance, are still very much alive in this rural area of the southern province. Age old folk songs, such as *Tia Anica* or *Ana from Loulé*, that celebrate the beauty of the land, and ballads recounting tales of local legendary figures are familiar to everyone. The frenetic *corridinho* – the fastest of all Portuguese dances – is danced energetically by young and old alike. Many of the inland communities have their own *rancho folclórico*. These traditional dance groups gather together each week in an explosion of colour and energy. Girls flutter their long patterned dresses, giving glimpses of their embroidered petticoats underneath. Their heads are wrapped

in silk or woollen scarves held fast with little hats. Their partners sport slim and elegant woollen trousers with spotless white shirts, tucked in and bound with red sashes. Flat, stiff hats complete the look, though these usually end up around their necks as they are spun off during the wild dancing.

A wonderful variety of colourful costumes can be seen during the local festivals. Strict dress codes are followed and the traditional clothes are worn exactly as they would have been back in the days when they were everyday wear.

LOULÉ

(**F5/H-I5**) ★ ✪ Loulé (pop. 9000) is one of the oldest towns in the region. It is the centre of the Algarvian craft industry and receives a constant influx of visitors from the outlying villages and beyond, who come here to do their shopping. Although it is only 12 km from the coast, it shares many of the characteristics and much of the charm of the inland villages. The maze of narrow alley-ways

Silves and its Moorish castle. Formerly a major trading centre, first established by the Phoenicians, Silves today is a fast growing town

lined with tall compact houses contrasts with an expansive boulevard shaded by rows of trees, which in spring burst into pinky-red blossom. The architecture of the Avenida, as it is called, is predominantly modern, but where it narrows there are still a handful of more traditional buildings decorated with ornate gables. Right in the middle of this flamboyant street stands the *coreto* (bandstand), where the local fire brigade band perform regular Sunday recitals. The *Bombeiros,* as they are known, are also renowned for their spectacular Christmas cribs that are proudly displayed in the local town hall. During the festive season, people come here from miles around to admire them.

The Moorish castle that dominates the town with its thick boundary walls is a proud and imposing structure. Today it houses the tourist office and a museum. The town has many reminders of the rich heritage that the Arabs left behind, but curiously, very little remains from the medieval period which followed the defeat of the Moors (by Paio Peres Correia who ran them out in 1249) and the subsequent establishment of Portuguese rule. The *Convento da Graça* and the *Convento do Francisco* are all that remains of significance. Both buildings have recently been restored and are now used as an exhibition hall and an art school respectively. Some of the stone features of these old convents were used in the renovation of other churches.

But the main attraction here is the market. Wander through the whitewashed houses that line the cobbled streets of the *Bairro Popu-*

lar. In this part of the old town you can watch the local craftsmen at work in their open workshops: see saddlers sewing waxed thread through hand cut leather, coppersmiths hammering white hot metal into shape, potters turning jugs from local clay and painting them with traditional designs. This lively centre of cottage industry is situated between the fortified walls and the Moorish castle. If you then walk through the solid gateway and beneath the *Câmara* tower (which houses the town hall) you will reach the *Praça da República.* This square is the heart and soul of Loulé and constantly pulsates with life. Traders are concentrated in the large market hall. With its arabesque windows and gates, and the mixture of smells, sounds and colours, the atmosphere is distinctly Oriental. Saturday is the busiest day in the week, when all the fresh fruit, vegetables, fish, and live game are brought in from all over the district to be sold. One corner of the hall is devoted to arts and crafts stalls, where you can buy all manner of handmade objects, for example sheepskin slippers, painted pottery and miscellaneous items fashioned from leather and wood. Many stalls overspill into the surrounding alleyways. By Sunday the swarms of bargain hunters and bus loads of tourists are gone, leaving the town in a state of relative calm.

SIGHTSEEING

Capela de Senhora da Piedade
This domed whitewashed chapel is dedicated to the patron saint of the Algarve. It stands on

MARCO POLO SELECTION: THE INTERIOR

1 La Réserve
Portugal's most romantic Hotel in Santa Barbara de Nexe – has an excellent restaurant (page 69)

2 Loulé
This ancient Moorish town is the centre of the crafts industry where you can

relax, after an exhausting spending spree, in the swimming pool or sauna (page 63)

3 Serra de Monchique
This isolated mountain region, full of tropical flowers and the scent of eucalyptus trees, is the Algarve's garden of Eden (page 69)

a hill just outside the town on the road to Boliqueime. In the annual *Mãe Soberana* procession, which falls on the second Sunday after Easter, the statue of Our Lady of Piety is carried up to her sanctuary. Local parishioners fill the chapel with heavily scented flowers, and it sparkles with the flames of votive candles, each of which carries a prayer of thanksgiving or supplication. The view from here of the surrounding countryside stretches for miles, over the orange groves, across the mountains, and out to sea.

Igreja Matriz
This parish church is situated in the old town on the *Largo Cabrito de Silva*. The *Capela das Almas* (Chapel of Alms) within has some beautiful azulejos laid out beyond a Renaissance portal.

Igreja de Misericórdia
There are four streets that lead off the *Praça da República* in the heart of town. Along the *Avenida Marçal Pacheco* which heads south-east towards Faro, just where the shops come to an end, is the church of Misericórdia, marked by an elegant granite cross that hangs over its door.

Nossa Senhora de Conceição
This little chapel is sandwiched between the houses and shops that line the road leading up to the castle. Inside it is cool and peaceful, and although a bit run down it has some impressive 200-year-old azulejos that depict the life of the Virgin Mary. The beautifully carved gilt altar dates from the 18th century.

CAFÉS & RESTAURANTS

O Avenida
Wonderful dishes steamed and served in the traditional *cataplana*. Tastefully decorated rooms. For a quick snack, try the snack bar next door.
Mon-Sat; Avenida José da Costa Mealha 7-13; Tel: 62106; Category 2

Avenida Velha
A homely restaurant decorated with family photos and typical Portuguese ornaments. Before placing your order, sample some of the delicious home-made appetizers such as the pickled sardines or grilled sausages. The service is very friendly.
Above the Shell Garage, Avenida José da Costa Mealha 40; Tel: 416 735; Category 2-3

Café Louletana

◈ An old established coffee house frequented by the men of Loulé in true oriental tradition.
On the main street between the castle and market place

Muralha

Restaurant in an original house in the old town. Serves Portuguese specialities.
Daily (except Tues); Rua Martim Moniz 41; Tel: 412 629; Category 2

Piccola Itália

Good Italian cooking in comfortable surroundings. Restaurant is on the first floor.
Daily (except Sun); Solar das Palmeiras (Five minutes walk from the market roundabout); Tel: (mobile) 0931/566 498; Category 2

Gelateria Portas do Céu

⚲ 'Heaven's Gates' serves the best ice-cream money can buy. Coffee and cake is also available.
Portas do Céu

SHOPPING

Loulé is a good place to find gifts and souvenirs. Browse through the craft shops along the ancient street of saddlers and coppersmiths – *Rua da Barbaça*. In amongst the fine leather saddles and quality harnesses you will find some lovely braids and trimmings – originally designed to ornament donkeys' reins, they make nice decorative souvenirs. Bells of all shapes and sizes can be bought from the coppersmiths, who also turn their hands to *cataplanas,* cutlery, and other copper and brass utensils. The central market (*mornings only*) is another good place to shop. There are stalls brimming with painted pots, wooden toys, hand-woven carpets, etc.

O Arco

Quality ceramics are turned and painted here. Personalized designs can be made to order, with inscriptions if desired.
Rua das Almadas

Dumela Africa

Imported handicrafts, jewellery, and minerals, mainly from Kenya and the former Portuguese colonies in Africa.
Avenida José da Costa Mealha 23

Modelo

Big, modern well-stocked supermarket, with fresh bread daily.
Daily 09.00- 20.00 hrs; Rua Olivais Santo António

HOTELS

Loulé Jardim Hotel

This is the only official hotel in Loulé. In a fine old town house, recently renovated, on the edge of a small park.
52 rooms; Praça Manuel de Arriaga. Tel: 413 094/95, Fax: 463 177; Category 2

Pensão Restaurante Avenida

A basic guest house with 12 rooms, six of which have a bathroom. Under the same management as the restaurant Avenida Velha above the Shell garage.
Avenida José da Costa Mealha 40; Tel: 416 735 or 416 474; Category 3

Residencial Dom Payo

26 modern rooms, all with bathroom en-suite.
Rua Antero Quent (parallel to the Avenida); Tel: 41 44 22; Category 2

Loulé has an excellent public swimming pool; just follow the signs for the *piscina*. The surrounding area is ideal for hiking.

INFORMATION

Posto de Turismo
Daily 09.00-19.00 hrs; Edifício do Castelo; Tel: 46 39 00

SURROUNDING AREA

Alte   (E4/H4)
❋ ◁/▷ 'At the foot of the four mountains, whence the water comes that feeds the wheel of the mill, thus spreading the song of the source, that is where the little village of Alte lies.' This is how the poet Cândido Guerreiro described his home town and, when not inundated with tour buses, it remains a typical Algarve village with a wonderful variety of flowers that seem to blossom eternally among the splashing fountains and white tiled houses.

Behind the small *Ermida de São Luís* flows a freshwater spring, the *Fonte das Bicas,* by a path that leads to a monument of Guerreiro, that bears a plaque inscribed with his poems. A pleasant place to sit and relax is beside the town's biggest natural water source, known as the *Grande Fonte*. ❋ This is where the locals like to congregate for a chat. It is particularly lively on 1 May, the spring festival. A big procession of flowers winds its way through the streets of Alte, filling them with colour. This is followed by a communal picnic by the spring. Everybody takes a bottle of fresh water home with them as it is said to contain special healing properties. Once you have quenched your thirst here, you can satisfy your hunger at the restaurant opposite which offers a good selection of quality dishes. The source of the spring is actually on the restaurant premises and known as the *Olho de Boi* (eye of an ox). Another aquatic attraction is the waterfall of *Pego no Vigário,* situated at the back of a small cemetery. Ask one of the locals for directions: most know where it is. For cave enthusiasts the *Sobradinho* is worth a visit. Situated near the road to Serra dos Soidos, the caves here have some impressive stalagmites. The festival of *São Luís,* patron saint of Alte, takes place in February at the same time as the sausage festival, *Festa dos Chouriços,* celebrated in thanksgiving to the saint, who is also the patron saint of animals, for keeping the pigs healthy and fat. Alte is also inhabited by a number of artists and craftspeople. There is a group of women toy-makers in Alte de Torre who have established a very good reputation for their skilled handiwork.

◁/▷ *Hotel Alte* offers a commanding view of the hills, valleys, and coastline. Sports facilities include a swimming pool, minigolf, and tennis courts. A bus service to the beach is also available for residents. *24 rooms; Tel: 68523/24, Fax: 68646; Category 2*

Mosteiro de Mú   (F3/H3)
◁/▷ About 3 km along the road from Salir in the direction of Benafim there is a turn off on the right that leads up to Malhão. This road takes you right up into the heart of the Serra do Caldeirão mountains. After a

steep climb of about 11 km, you will sight the fluttering prayer flags of a Buddhist monastery in the distance. This is the Humkaradzong Centre, an extraordinary sanctuary built on a high plateau. It is inhabited by about 30 Tibetan monks and their families. A cluster of simply built houses cling to the hillside just below the plateau. The large circular tent you will see is reserved for prayer. The surrounding scenery is quite Himalayan in that you do feel as if you are on the roof of the world. It is especially breathtaking when the setting sun casts its pastel shades across the valley. The monastery is on private land that is closed to the public, but you can come here to meditate. *Tel: 414 728*

Querença (F4/I4)

NP The high country begins between Loulé and Barranco do Velho. The landscape is one of rolling foothills and the mountains beyond. The hilltops are mostly bare, but the steep inclines are covered in rich vegetation; wild roses and strawberry bushes run riot. The valley floors are also very fertile, irrigated by the many small rivers that flow through them. Half way between Loulé and Barranco, about 10 km up into these hills, is Querença. Perched on a hilltop, the focal point of the village is its church, which stands on the highest point. It is a modest looking house of worship, but has some hidden treasures inside, such as the baptismal font, and above the gate a unique example of Algarvian naïve painting depicting a group of saints. The church stands before a beautiful square

that is both spacious and serene, and is a lovely spot to stop and contemplate the surrounding country. On the first floor of the house next door is a restaurant with a **NP** compelling view. The De Querença, as it is called, is particularly busy on Saturday nights when live performances are given by accordion players. *(Largo da Igreja; Tel: 422 540; reservation recommended; Category 2).* If you want to stop over for a night try the *Quinta da Várzea (Tel: 414 443, Fax: 422 055; Category 2).*

Not far from Querença are two stalagmite caves, the subject of many a mysterious tale. Further out is the *Benémola spring*, a favourite picnic spot among the locals.

Salir (F4/H4)

Formerly an impregnable settlement protected by the thick boundary walls and castle (Castelo de Salir), today Salir is a peaceful village. There are only a few scattered remains of the ancient stronghold, among which cabbages have taken root. It is worth a visit purely for the ==beautiful and untouched landscape,== and the fresh air that blows down from the mountains. The *Festa das Espigas*, the 'corn cob festival' held in February, breaks the stillness with its lively celebrations. It often coincides with the popular sausage festival.

NP The village church is fairly unremarkable, but before it spreads a spectacular view. On one side are the mountains of Barranco do Velho and on the other the rolling hills of Loulé. Towering up to the side is the Cerro dos Negros (474 m) which forms part of the Macacos range. To the north-west is the similarly tall (479 m) Rocha de Pena, at the base of which are the 'Moorish caves', a labyrinth of inter-connecting chambers, good for an adventurous afternoon's exploration.

Santa Bárbara de Nexe   (I 5)

Because of its prime location, many foreigners have settled in this village over the years. Only 7 km from Loulé and 12 km from Faro, it has all the necessary conveniences to hand, such as the small local airport, beaches, golf courses, and shops, without the tourist chaos. Highly popular and well-recommended is the region's only hotel. It is a romantic place to stay, and the service is as excellent as it is discreet. Bask in the gardens and enjoy the fresh, clean air, relax by the pool, or sweat it out on the tennis courts. Under the same roof is one of the Algarve's best restaurants, famed for its high class cuisine. ★ *Hotel and Restaurant La Réserve; Santa Bárbara de Nexe; Tel: 90474 and 90234, Fax: 90402; Category L*

Apartments with balcony and pool are available for families or groups of 4-5. Contact the Niehoffs at *Santa Bárbara de Nexe; Tel: 90848; Category 2*

SERRA DE MONCHIQUE

(C4) ★ ⚘ An oasis of green, abundant with flowers and flowing waters where women do their washing as turtles swim up and down. Just one rural snapshot of many from the isolated mountain region of Monchique. This wall of hills, reaching up to around 900 m, shields the south from the cool north winds, thus maintaining the temperate climate the Algarve is so renowned for. Within the Serra itself a unique micro climate prevails, favouring a unique mixture of tropical, subtropical and north European flora. Banana trees, wood anemones and yams co-exist in this fertile environment, its richness underlined by the splendid colours of the ubiquitous camellias.

The mountain region of the Serra de Monchique – a lush and fertile landscape, perfect for hiking

A 30 km drive from Silves along the shaded road, past the marble quarry and through the eucalyptus and cork-oak forests (that stand out from amid the surrounding vegetation with their freshly peeled orange trunks), brings you to Caldas de Monchique. The thermal baths

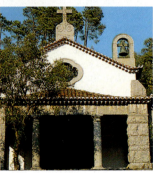

Caldas de Monchique, where time seems to have stood still

are the main attraction of this sleepy spa town that has remained relatively unspoilt over the years. The central square is furnished with tables and chairs that stand beneath the shade of plane trees, and is a great place to relax. Art nouveau houses complement buildings from the Belle Epoque, creating a romantic, fin-de-siècle atmosphere.

The thermal water (32°) is said to alleviate all forms of rheumatism, skin and stomach disorders. Roman emperors and Portuguese kings took the cure here and the aura of old Portugal still hangs in the air. The baths are open between 1 June and 15 November. There are footpaths that lead from the baths into the surrounding woods; perfect for a peaceful, refreshing stroll. Follow the

stream and you will be rewarded with great panoramic views from the *Mirante, Quinta de Belle-France,* and *Volta da Vagarosa.* The best place to stay in the vicinity is at the *Albergaria do Lageado; 20 rooms; Tel: 92616; Category 2*

A further 200 m uphill lies the town of Monchique (pop. 7000), renowned for its *medronho,* a strong, clear, sweet spirit that is made from the fruit of the *arbutus* bush, indigenous to the region. The berries from this plant are not edible, but once distilled they make a wonderful drink. This 'fire water' is sold all over Monchique, where you can even buy it by the barrel. Other regional gastronomic delights include *presunto* (cured ham), *frangos* (small chickens), and a local aromatic *mel* (honey), all of which are widely available.

The parish church is also worth a closer look. Built in the Manueline style, the portal is a particularly imaginative feature. Two corkscrew columns intertwined like a knotted rope are crowned by five turban-shaped structures. Inside the church there are some attractive wood carvings and azulejos.

Another distinctive architectural structure is the *Nossa Senhora de Desterro.* This former Franciscan monastery, built in 1632, dominates the town. The bell tower still stands tall, but the main building is now a ruin, though glimpses of its former glory can be seen in the Renaissance and arabesque detail of its remains. You can climb to the top of the bell tower, which offers a view across the colourful landscape of gardens and fruit plantations of Monchique. In spring the clock-tower is particularly beautiful as it glows from the blossom of the nearby gigantic magnolia tree. A coat of arms is still visible on the monastery façade. It was founded by Dom Pedro de Silvas, who later became Viceroy of the Indies. A stone's throw away is the *Fonte dos Pastorinhos* (the 'fountain of little shepherds') beautifully decorated with old tiles.

In fine weather, the walk up the winding road to 🌿 *Fóia*, at the summit of the Serra de Monchique, is worth the effort. The path is signposted from the market square. Half way up, you can have a break and a bite to eat in one of the *tascas* along the road. These eateries serve traditional dishes on the terraces that overlook the valley. Further up, the wood starts to thin out, and right at the top there is a wide clearing. The summit is marked by a kind of obelisk and some radio masts. The all-encompassing panorama from here is hard to beat. Hills and mountains roll smoothly down to the southern sea. On a clear day you can see across to the Alentejo region, and as far as the Sintra mountains next to Lisbon. If you wish to enjoy the view at sunset you can stay at the

Estalagem Abrigo da Montanha (10 rooms), Corte Pereira/Estrada de Fóia; Tel: 92131 Fax: 93660; Category 2

SILVES

(**D4**) Sung about by poets, lauded and loved by kings and princes, and sought after by their enemies, Silves was once the richest and most important town in the Algarve – at least according to local history books. One look at the red sandstone fortress which towers majestically over the town, and you will certainly believe it. The streets leading up to this imposing structure are lined with blue, yellow and white painted houses. On entering the courtyard through a plain and narrow gate you are transported into the past. There is a statue at the castle entrance of Dom Sancho I, the so-called 'liberator' of the city, which he delivered from its Moorish rulers in the name of Christianity. At that time it was known as Xelb, its Arabic name, with a reputation of being 'stronger, more beautiful, and ten times more important than Lisbon'. The last Moorish king of Al-Gharb, Mutadit Ibn Abad of Seville, gave his son, Mutamid,

The enchanted castle

The great cisterns that lie beneath the castle grounds are shrouded in myth. They are purported to have enchanted sources. The Cisterna dos Cães, for example, is said to be connected to the river Arade by a secret underground tunnel, while the Cisterna da Moura draws its water from a gigantic underground cavern, where five galleons are said to lie at anchor. The tale goes that at full moon a beautiful black-haired woman with a dark brown face floats across the reservoir in a schooner, and sings songs which, if you could hear them, would break your heart.

sovereignty over Xelb. This was a prosperous period and the town became the political, economic, and cultural focal point of the Algarve. Poets and princes held court here and decided the province's future.

Back then Silves boasted a population of at least 30 000 (three times the number of its present inhabitants). Its geographical situation on the fast flowing Arade river could not have been better. Cork, eucalyptus wood, pomegranates, figs and almonds were shipped from here to the Arab lands of northern Africa. Palaces and town houses were built around the castle walls, and in the vicinity Arab traders, renowned for their business acumen, set up their tents. Little evidence remains of this thriving commercial settlement, but a stroll along the castle battlements affords an impressive view. You can see the Arade running its course through fertile fields, bursting with almond blossoms in spring and oranges in summer. It flows on under the seven-arched Roman bridge and south through the town, down towards the sea.

The Monchique mountains in the north-west form a chain that surrounds the town, and are known as The Heads of Silves (*Cabeças de Silves*), the two main peaks being Monte Branco in the north and Monte de Jóia to the south. In the cooler months, a trek through the hills is a good way to escape the traffic and chaos of tourism and find peace and quiet in the middle of some stunning scenery.

Looking out from the castle in a south-easterly direction you

Cruz de Portugal, the limestone crucifix on the outskirts of Silves

will see the old cork factory in the valley, which is still in operation today. In the castle itself, or rather beneath it, are two massive water tanks installed hundreds of years ago, which, until recently, held most of Silves' water supply. They are known as the *Cisterna da Moura* and *Cisterna dos Cães* (The Cistern of the Moorish Woman and the Dogs' Cistern). They are ventilated through manholes which emerge in the castle's main courtyard. In 1189, the King of Portugal, Sancho I, with the assistance of English and German crusaders, launched an attack on Xelb. His first attempt to capture the citadel failed, but his small army reduced the outlying settlements to ash and rubble. The battle raged on, and for six weeks Xelb withstood the siege. Then on 3 September 1189 the Moors were finally defeated and Dom Sancho I proclaimed himself 'King of Portugal and the Algarve'. The period immediately following his victory was prosperous but short-lived. The vital River Arade silted up (the same fate that befell the royal Moorish town Tavira on the river Gilão), resulting in a rapid reduction of the town's economic power. But

Silves' final downfall came in 1755 with the great earthquake.

Despite such relentless destruction, Silves boasts South Portugal's oldest church, the Sé. This striking Gothic cathedral, which has three naves and is made from red sandstone, was built on the foundations of a mosque and was the bishopric of the Algarve until 1577. King João II was initially buried here. Though his body was subsequently moved to Batalha, his tombstone next to the altar still remains. Other interesting interior features include the Torre de Caracol (the spiral tower) and the *holy water fonts*, carved out of local stone, as is the statue of the Virgem de Pedra (Virgin of Stone) who is carried in a festival procession held in her honour.

The *Ermida da Nossa Senhora dos Mártires* was once a sacred burial ground for soldiers who were killed in battle within the city walls. In the south of the town is the ancient city gate, the *Arco da Rebola* (next to the Misericórdia church); and just by the Silves exit road, as you head in the direction of São Bartolomeu de Messines, stands the *Cruz de Portugal*. Carved in limestone in the Manueline style by an unknown artist, this 3 m-high cross represents on one side the Crucifixion of Christ, and on the other the Deposition (the taking down of Christ from the cross).

RESTAURANT

O Rui

This *marisqueira* (seafood restaurant), right in the heart of Silves, has gained a good reputation for its fresh fish and shellfish dishes, which can be ordered in normal or half size (*meia dose*) portions. Attracts locals, and tourists from all over the Algarve.
Daily (except Tues); Rua Comendador Villurinho; Tel: 442 682; Category 2

HOTEL

Residencial Castelo

Attractive rooms in a comfortable atmosphere. Next door to the castle.
Largo 1 de Maio; Tel: 42316; Category 2

ENTERTAINMENT

Café Inglés

This lively bar at the foot of the castle is the central place to meet in the evening. It has a cool roof garden and holds frequent live music performances.
Daily (except Sun) from 19.00 hrs

INFORMATION

Posto de Turismo

Mon-Sat 09.00-13.00 and 15.00-19.00 hrs; Rua 25 de Abril; Tel: 42255

SURROUNDING AREA

Arade Reservoir (D4)

In spite of the numerous tents and caravans that are pitched all around the lake, the *Barragem do Arade* reservoir is well worth a visit. Lying about 10 km outside the town, it contains enough fresh water to supply Silves during the dry summer months. It is set in a beautiful and very diverse landscape. Water-skiing and windsurfing facilities are provided on the lake.

Home of the great explorers

A dramatic coastline, isolated and wild

This is the westernmost region of Europe and the last two towns along its coast before the vast expanse of the Atlantic are Lagos and Portimão. Given its situation at the edge of a continent, the port of Lagos, constantly buffeted by fresh sea breezes, naturally became a town of seafarers, and was home to many of the great explorers who made Portugal into such an important centre during the Renaissance. It was from here that some of the first expedition fleets to Africa and Asia departed and, to the town's shame, it was also the first town in Europe to sell slaves that these 'pioneers' brought back with them. Portimão (pop. 26 000), which lies at the mouth of the Arade River, is the capital of the west, and is the second most important town in the Algarve after Faro. At the turn of the century it was amongst the top holiday destinations favoured by Europe's élite, largely because it boasts one of the most beautiful beaches in the Algarve, the Praia da Rocha.

LAGOS

(C5) Despite a history spanning 2500 years, Lagos (pop. 10 000) is a youthful, dynamic and cosmopolitan town. Popular with young tourists, many of whom have taken up residence here, it is certainly a lively place to be, with an abundance of bars and restaurants of every nationality.

Lagos is 40 km from Cabo de São Vicente and 90 km from Faro airport; and the railway line that runs along the coast from Vila Real de Santo António on the Spanish border terminates here. The Baia, or Bay, of Lagos is a unique geographical feature neatly divided by the Alvor River delta. Many regard it as one of the most beautiful bays in Europe. The town beach is the Meia Praia, which runs westwards in a bold curve up to the Ponta da Piedade. Venture a little further afield and you will discover secluded bays and small hidden beaches. Because of the strong sea currents

The lighthouse at Cabo de São Vicente has the most powerful beam in Europe

75

the beaches are always changing shape: the Praia Dona Ana, for example, has gradually narrowed and now, at high tide, it divides into two beaches, separated by a strip of calm water.

Formerly known as Lacóbriga in Roman times, this was the town where Henry the Navigator was born. During his reign, Lagos became the gateway to the world. He dreamt of 'entering into the unknown' and sent armadas to sea to 'discover' new lands, and thus began the era of Portuguese colonization. Gil Eanes, also from Lagos, was the first man to circumnavigate the Cape of Bojador, giving Henry the proof he needed for his theory that the world did not end at the *mare tenebrosum* (the sea of darkness) as was formerly believed. The list of Henry's achievements is long. He established a marine college in Sagres, and was present during every stage of planning for a new voyage of discovery. He made studies of the sea currents and wind patterns and, with a team of scientists, cartog-

raphers, and astrologists, formulated incredibly detailed maps of the sea, perfected navigational aids like the compass and the astrolabe, and built prototypes of new ships. He personally tutored ships' captains and taught them to navigate by the stars. He tried to promote a sceptical, empirical philosophy, one in which facts were founded upon proof, not tradition and belief. Ironically, he rarely sailed himself – his qualities lay in the discovery of the unrecognized connection, the intuitive leap, and a passionate desire to extend the boundaries of the world. With so many preoccupations he had little time to enjoy the good things in life. This perhaps explains the rather serious, thoughtful expression on the commemorative statue of him that stands in front of Lagos fort.

Although Sagres was the academic centre, Lagos was the place where theory was put into practice and ideas were brought to fruition. Great ships were built here and sent on long voyages around the world. They brought back treasures that had never been seen before: spices, ivory, sugar, and all sorts of precious metals. The slave trade also flourished during this period — what is now the customs office was once a massive slave market. Trading in people was a new phenomenon and caught on not only because the labour was cheap, but also because Africans were regarded as a curiosity.

Inspired by the writings of Marco Polo that he had read as a teenager, Henry the Navigator dreamed of exploring Ethiopia. This was one ambition he did not achieve, but he did become a model figure who inspired many explorers. In 1460 Dom Henrique o Navegador died in Sagres, and was buried in the church of Santa Maria in Lagos, but the building was destroyed in the great earthquake and his body was never retrieved. After his death, Portugal's reputation as a seafaring nation held strong for some 100 years during which time Vasco da Gama circumnavigated the Cape of Good Hope;

Pedro Alvares Cabral conquered Brazil; Goa, Java, Ceylon and Canton became Portuguese colonies; and Ferdinand Magellan sailed around the tip of South America (Magellan's Strait) and crossed an ocean he named the Pacific. This era came to an end shortly after Mendes Pinto's historic journey to Japan and the disappearance of the young King Sebastião (1554-1578). He dreamed of defeating Islam and set off with some 20 000 crusaders to fight the great Alcácer Kebir. It turned out to be a suicide mission from which only 60 survivors sailed home. Despite this massacre, the Portuguese still have a distinct nostalgia for the times in which they had, or hoped for, mastery of the waves. In the 17th century Lagos Bay was the scene of great sea battles between the world powers of the day: the Dutch and English (allies of Spain) fought against the might of the French navy here and, in keeping with the transient alliances of the day, it was only a few years later, in 1797, that England came to fight

The harbour town of Lagos, over 2500 years old, is as young and active as ever

Spain in the same place. At the beginning of the 19th century, French domination came to an end, and Portuguese were set against Portuguese when the Liberals revolted against the monarchist supremacy in the bloody battle of Lagos in 1833. The town still shows signs of this tumultuous period. Parts of the city wall can still be seen, and on the *Praça da República* stand a handful of buildings which date back to this time: the *Governor's Palace,* which still bears its old coat of arms and now houses the town hospital; the tranquil façade of the *Customs Office,* under whose arches slaves were auctioned, belies its unpleasant history. The *aqueduct* in the old town was built between 1490 and 1521. Although much of it has been destroyed, Lagos nevertheless maintains its 19th-century character.

SIGHTSEEING

Igreja de Santo António
This church was rebuilt in 1769, after the earthquake. Above the azulejo pulpit is an exquisite example of late baroque gilt woodcarving, complemented by 18th-century paintings. The statue of Santo António, flanked by large angels, is draped in a red officer's sash, allegedly offered to him by the Crusaders for helping them to victory.
Rua General Alberto Silveira

Lagos Marina
This new marina. is worth a visit. It is overlooked by the 17th-century *Ponta da Bandeira* fort, which stands opposite the town gates. The city wall complex is some 100 years older and once formed

part of the slave market. Today it houses an art gallery.

Ponta da Piedade
★ The most southerly point of Lagos Bay is a 20 m-tall cliff face. A spectacular landscape of extraordinary rock formations, caverns and columned grottoes. The *Ponta da Piedade* is best viewed from the sea, and boat tours are offered by the local fishermen for around £4.00 per person. Departures from the *Ponta da Piedade* or from the new *Lagos Marina.* The tourist office and some of the hotels also organize day trips with a picnic lunch included.

MUSEUMS

Museu Municipal
This informative and evocative museum is next to the church of St Anthony. Its exhibits include archaeological finds, pre-Roman artefacts and Roman mosaics, weaponry and models of ships.
Mon-Fri 09.30-12.30 and 14.00-17.00 hrs; Rua General Alberto Silveira

RESTAURANTS

The town offers a real diversity of cuisines.

Adega da Marina
Traditionally, an *adega* is a place for drinking wine, but in this particular estabishment they serve good food too. Opposite the new harbour.
Avenida dos Descobrimentos 35; Category 3

No Patio
Tucked away behind a green door in the Old Town, this Swedish-

run restaurant serves good evening meals on the patio.
Daily (except Mon); Rua Lançarote de Freitas 46; Tel: 763 777; Category 1-2

O Poço

10 km from Lagos in the direction of Sagres is the small village of Almadena. This small bar and restaurant stands on the main square. The food and service are excellent.
Tel: 69433; Category 2

SHOPPING

Antique shop

Brimming with miscellaneous objects, including an impressive collection of crucifixes. Just look for the chattering parrot that is permanently stationed at the entrance.
Rua 25 de Abril

Leoa

A mixture of classic and avantgarde art and fashion.
Rua Vasco da Gama 43

Mogador

African shop full of Berber jewellery and leather goods.
Rua Gil Eanes

Terra a Vista

Nicely decorated shop/exhibition space run by a couple who make their own African style sculptures, specializing in birds and animals.
Marina

HOTELS

There is a wide choice of accommodation on offer in and around Lagos. The two main camp-sites

Lagos is dotted with small squares that lend the town centre grace and charm

are *Campismo Imulagos* and *Campismo Rossio da Trindade.*

Albergaria Casa de São Gonçalo

A well-kept hostel in a listed house.
13 rooms; Rua Cândido dos Reis 81; Tel: 762 171, Fax: 763 927; Category 1

Pensão Residencial Sol e Praia

Right next to the beach, and nice and quiet.
105 rooms; Praia Dona Ana; Tel: 762 026, Fax: 760 247; Category 1

São Cristovão

Mid-range hotel on the outskirts of town.
77 rooms; Avenida dos Descobrimentos; Tel: 763 051, Fax: 763 054; Category 2

SPORT & LEISURE

The best area for surfing and wind-surfing is on the long beach of *Meia Praia*, especially after 16:00 hrs when the wind direction turns seaward. The nearby hotels all rent out boards. Sunbathers are advised to stick to the beaches that are protected by cliffs, as the sand on exposed beaches flies about when the wind picks up. *Clube de Vela* is a sailing club where watersports enthusiasts meet; diving schools are centred around the *Praia de Luz,* and they usually hire out equipment as well. The best dive sites can only be reached by boat, but visibility is not always good. The most sheltered beach is on the west side of the Baia de Lagos about 3 km from the town centre. You can go horse-riding on the beach at the *Centro Equestre da Atalaya,* Atalaya beach. The nearest golf course is in Palmares (*Tel: 762 953*). For a bird's eye view of the Algarve try a Microlight trip. *Lagos airport; Tel: 762 906*

ENTERTAINMENT

Given its predominantly young population, Lagos is not short of bars and clubs . ✪ The *Adega Bar Mullins* (*Ruâ Cândido dos Reis*) is frequented by locals of all ages. It is run by two Scots who play a mixture of jazz and reggae, with some Ella Fitzgerald thrown in, and serve a minimal but good selection of food up to 23.00 hrs. There is a dance floor, and the place starts to get really lively towards midnight. Down in the bay there are numerous beach bars which vary in style and quality. The *Berlim Bar* is one of the better ones. It serves tasty grilled snacks and enjoys a cool sea breeze (*opposite the Meia Praia Hotel*). After supper time all the fado singers begin to do their rounds, and the *Mouralha* next to the city wall

always has good performances. ♟ The trendiest and most original venue is *O Pôr do Sol.* It is run by Dino, the Angolan owner, and draws an interesting mix of local Portuguese and Angolans and international travellers. The food is basic and not particularly exciting, but that's not what people come here for. They gather and chat around the bar and pool tables, and the atmosphere is convivial. It is not really recommended for families, but if you want a lively night out go along late. It's situated right at the end of the beach, just past the railway lines.

INFORMATION

Posto de Turismo
Mon-Sat 09.00-19.00 hrs, Sun 09.00-17.00 hrs; Largo Marquês de Pombal; Tel: 763031

SURROUNDING AREA

Barragem da Bravura   (B-C4)
Ideal for fishing and picnicking, this reservoir is filled with fresh water from the Monchique mountains. Take the road to Lisbon from Lagos and after about 5 km take the turn-off signposted to *Colinas Verdes.*

Boca do Rio   (B5)
This beach (which contains the remains of an ancient Roman fishery) is about 15 km from Lagos and is, as yet, relatively free of tourists. The nearby *Salema beach* has a tough golf course.
Parque de Floresta, Vale do Poço, Budens; Tel: 65333

O Cangalho   (B5)
This farm right out in the sticks belongs to the local surrealist

painter Paulo. It is in Medronhal, a small village on the road between Barão de São João and Bensafrim, and is open to the public from 11.00 hrs until late at night, and serves snacks, drinks and hearty rustic cuisine.
Daily (except Mon); Tel: 67218; Category 2

Mata da Barão de São João   (B5)
This coastal wood is a beautiful spot for hiking. To get there, take the main road to Barão de São João and turn left at the village entrance (by the fountain). Carry on up the road into the heart of the forest. You can park outside the Florestal restaurant and guest house *(daily, except Tues; Category 2)*. There are a number of different hiking routes that set off from here.

Raposeira/Casa do Infante   (A-B5)
The house in which Henry the Navigator is said to have lived is just 1 km from Vila do Bispo on the N 125. Annexed to it is the *Nossa Senhora de Guadalupe* chapel, which was his personal place of meditation and prayer. Ask for the keys at the grocer's on the village square (a tip would not go unappreciated). The chapel was built by the Knights Templar in the 13th century and is thought to be the oldest Christian house of worship in the Algarve. Nearby is a good family hotel: *Pensão Mira Sagres in Vila do Bispo; 5 rooms; Tel: 66160; Category 3*. Very basic, but spotlessly clean. The service is friendly, and the landlady is a marvellous cook.

Torre de Aspa   (A5)
The highest cliffs in the Algarve are just 3 km west of Vila do Bispo, towering 156 m above Castelo beach, where an assortment of fascinating pebbles are scattered over the sand. These sparkling stones, polished by the sea, are marbled with subtle colours and veined with grey and white lines.

West Coast   (B3-4)
North of Sagres the coastal waters become a bit wilder and, although very beautiful, are too dangerous for swimming. The sea is calmer around *Amoreira* and *Monte Clérigo* north of Aljezur. *Carrapateira* and *Bordeira* are a surfer's paradise, and have wide expansive stretches of sand. It's a short hike to *Arrifana,* where the ruins of an ancient fort stand. The *Ponta da Atalaia* dominates the landscape. For accommodation, try the *Hotel Vale da Telha; 26 rooms; Tel: 98180; Category 2,* or *Casa Fajara* in *Carrapateira; 9 rooms; Tel/Fax: 97123; Category 2*. Horses can be hired here too. Or, in *Monte Clérigo* you can stay at *José and Ilda Sabido's Urbanização do Espartal; Tel: 997 301; Category 3*. There is also a camp-site (*Campismo Vale da Telha)* between Carrapateira and Odeceixe, 5 minutes from the beach. *Aljezur* itself is nothing special, but the 12th century ✵ Moorish fort has an outstanding view.

PORTIMÃO

(**C5**) Portimão is the home of Portugal's largest sardine fishing fleet and canning factory. Every afternoon you can smell and hear the early morning catch sizzling away on charcoal grills all around town. Restaurants are always well stocked, catering for the hordes

The fishermen of Portimão repairing their nets

of hungry fishermen and travellers. In days gone by, the ships' hauls were passed from deck to quay by hundreds of helping hands. Unfortunately for the tourist (but probably not for the labourers) all the unloading is now mechanized, and this spectacle is a thing of the past. If you go to Ferragudo on the other side of the Arade bay, you might be lucky enough to witness traditional methods still being carried out. Portimão is a major commercial centre. The bustling streets are packed with small, well stocked shops. The town itself is not particularly attractive, but it does boast one of the best loved beaches of the Algarve — the Praia da Rocha.

CAFÉS & RESTAURANTS

There is no shortage of places to eat in Portimão, but typical of the area are the *tascas* where fresh sardines are grilled to perfection.

Pastelaria Almeida

Tea and coffee house run by two old ladies who serve a mouth watering selection of home-made cakes and pastries.
Largo 1 de Dezembro

Casa Inglesa

◉ This lively café is Portimão's central gossip spot — a popular meeting place for locals and tourists alike.
Largo Teixeira Gomes 3

Escondidinho

If you have worked up an appetite and need a good substantial meal, this restaurant, tucked away in the shopping centre, serves hearty rustic food.
Porta de São João; Category 3

Lúcio

A real favourite amongst the locals. Lúcio prepares the fish and shellfish himself.
Largo Serpa Pinto (opposite the sardine packers); Category 2-3

O Mané

With its bright blue tiled exterior this restaurant is difficult to miss. The interior is typically Portuguese and the cooking is good.
Take the Rua Júdice Biker towards town and veer right; Category 3

SHOPPING

Just behind the tourist office is the shopping district, made up of narrow alleys and pedestrianized areas. It's a lively place and you can find almost everything here. The prices are allegedly lower than in the rest of the Algarve. *Bobi* specializes in beautiful ceramic and pewter pieces, while *St James* sells good shoes and bags. There are many antique shops stocked with a wide variety of objects from old cupboards to antique tiles.

HOTELS

Hotel Globo

Well organized and clean with 80 rooms. Not recommended if you want peace and quiet as it is right in the middle of town.
Rua 5 de Outubro 26; Tel: 416 350, Fax: 83142; Category 2

Albergaria Miradoiro

The four stars are well deserved: the interior is very pretty and the service efficient and friendly.
32 rooms; Rua Machado dos Santos 13; Tel: 23011, Fax: 415 030; Category 1

SPORT & LEISURE

Perfect on those rare bad weather days, the CLCC halls offer a variety of classes including aerobics, ballet, body building, jazz dance and yoga. If you're feeling less energetic why not take some Portuguese lessons.
Jardim Gil Eanes; Tel: 416 496

ENTERTAINMENT

A lot of the bars here have British proprietors. Try the *Dennis Bar.* In an old converted house, it has a friendly atmosphere and often stages live music. Further afield, Ferragudo has some good jazz venues, or if you want just to hang out try the Praia da Rocha.

INFORMATION

Posto de Turismo

Daily 09.00-19.00 hrs; Largo 1 de Dezembro 33; Tel: 23695

SURROUNDING AREA

Alvor (C5)

Although surrounded by luxury houses and apartments this fishing village has kept itself modestly to itself. Along the coastline, however, runs 6 km of back to back giant tourist complexes, all the way from Alvor to Praia da Rocha. In the middle of all this is the *Praia do Vau*, which is renowned for its iodine-rich water and healthy clean air. The grand old house that stands on the cliff was the secondary residence of Mário Soares, Portugal's former president. Alvor village ★ is dependent on the river and estuary for its prosperity. It is a beautifully picturesque spot. Rare species of birds nest here, taking their pick of the rare delicacies that swim around in the shallows, and the lagoon is dotted with colourful fishing boats. Fishing is still a principal source of income and the auction halls and surrounding fishermen's bars and cafés are buzzing with activity. There are plenty of restaurants serving exquisite fresh fish dishes such as the *Fisherman's Rest (Daily, except Mon; Category 3)*. The *Grill Restaurant* in the luxury *Alvor Praia Hotel* is very stylish and open to non-residents. The rooms are well done out and overlook a lovely sandy beach *(217 rooms; Tel: 458 900, Fax: 458 999; Grill Restaurant, daily except Thurs; Category 2)*

Alvila on Tuesday nights is the place to go for authentic Fado *(1 km from Alvor on the road to Praia da Rocha; Tel: 458775; Category 2)*. The cuisine is both Algarvian and international. A short walk east of the Alvor Praia is *Prainha,* a modern well-designed resort with a luxurious round swimming pool, built by the *Três Irmãos* beach. The cliffs along its shore have been sculpted by the waves into ==unique rock formations== and the surrounding waters are rich with marine life, making this an ideal spot for snorkelling and diving. Boats can also be hired for fishing trips or visits to the grottoes from *José Carlos (Travessa da Igreja 1; approx. £15.00 per hour)*. He can also be contacted through a local bar *Tel: 449 102.*

Carvoeiro   (D5)

The road from Portimão to the Praia do Carvoeiro passes through Lagoa, the viticultural centre of the region. It's worth making a small detour to visit the wine cellars here. The regional wine is a little on the heavy side, but they do produce a good *aguardente.* This 'fire water' is a distilled drink, not unlike sherry, made from the remaining grape pressings. It is aged for at least five years in oak barrels, then bottled and stamped with the label *Aperitif Afonso III.* You can visit the cellars to see how it is made and for a tasting. If you want to stay on for a meal, the Belgian gourmet cuisine at *Chrissy's* is recommended. *(Daily except Mon; next to the church; Tel: 341 062; Category 1).*

Carvoeira is a popular resort in the same vein as Albufeira. It too has its roots in fishing, alongside the production of charcoal, a fuel which is widely used. It was once the favourite retreat of the wealthy élite from Lisbon and Lagoa who spent the four month summer season here, lounging in secluded bays, entertaining in their luxury bungalows, and frittering their money away in the casino. Nowadays, although it has maintained a certain exclusivity, it is mostly frequented by foreign tourists. ☟ There is a breathtaking view from the cliff-tops, and if you climb up the streets of the little port and look west to Sagres, the infinite waters you see beyond were once thought to be the end of the world.

★ At the bottom of a set of steps nearby is ==*Algar Seco*.== This magical world of rock pillars and archways is a geological marvel. Continuously changing colour in the sunlight as the day progresses, this labyrinth of natural sculptures changes shape constantly as the sea washes relentlessly in and out, splashing and bubbling over the soft limestone. A small lake lies within this rocky landscape, and its level rises and falls with the tide. On the top of the cliff stands *Parque Algar Seco* — a chic holiday complex equipped with

Smugglers Bay

Captain Carvalho is a name everyone knows in Alfanzina. An eccentric character who, around the turn of the century, built high walls and watch towers around his estate, the Quinta do Carvalho. So well guarded was his property that not even customs officers could set foot on his land. He had his own guarded harbour, warehouses and living quarters in Alfanzina, and was the talk of the town and the subject of much conjecture. It was widely believed that he was a smuggler and that his house was as filled with treasure as Ali Baba's cave. Still overlooked by an old watch tower, this pretty little beach is known to this day as Smuggler's Bay.

all mod cons. The imposing *Farol de Alfanzina lighthouse* along the coast is visible from here. Right next to it is another natural phenomenon in the form of a lava funnel that is still active. If you continue in this direction you will come to another holiday complex. Walk through it, past the dead end street, and you will find a path that leads through a tunnel and along a well-trodden path to the old *smugglers beach*. Here you'll see columns of rock rising out of the water, and the cliff you have just walked down from looms tall over the beach. This is a great picnic spot, but because of the high cliffs it gets direct sunlight only in the middle of the day.

There is a crop of Dutch, Portuguese, English, and German restaurants huddled together in town. At Chef António's, the fresh dishes come sizzling to your table. Preparation is a little slow, but it's worth the wait. The atmosphere is pleasant, and the prices are reasonable (*O Chefe António; Estrada do Farol; Tel: 358 937; Category 2-3*). Just around the corner is *O Cantinho*, renowned for its hearty Portuguese dishes (*Estrada do Farol; Tel: 358 234; Cat-egory 2-3*). *Centianes*, above the beach of the same name, is a good, comfortable restaurant run by a German artist (*Tel: 358 724; Category 1*). For a nice cool beer try *Flic Flac (daily from 18.00 hrs; Estrada do Farol 65, opposite O Chefe António).*

Hotels and apartments are available in every price range. If you want to splash out, there are a number of villas for rent, complete with pool and tennis court, even maids and gardeners. The *Carvoeiro Club* has some nice villas from around £80 a night, accommodating as many as ten people. *Tel: 357 266 Fax 357 725.*

Praia do Carvoeiro and its tiny fishing harbour

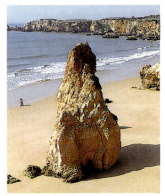

Praia da Rocha is renowned for its spectacular rock formations

◁▷ *Pension Baselli* overlooks the harbour. The service is friendly and you can treat yourself to a delicious balcony breakfast with fresh bread and home-made jam. They also have two apartments and a house with patio available for rent. *Tel: 357 159; Category 2*

Ferragudo   (D5)
Ferrugado lies on the left bank of the Arade, opposite Portimão. It is a simple but pictureque fishing village interlaced with little alleyways. A good camping spot, ideal for backpackers *(across the bridge and to the right)*.

Praia da Rocha   (C5)
Once the exclusive haunt of visiting British colonial officers, the elegance and traditionalism of this established resort have long since been wiped out by mass tourism. Many of the grand old villas were torn down to make way for modern hotels and apartment blocks. During the pre-War years Praia da Rocha was a select, high society resort and its most prestigious residence was the

Bela Vista. With its art nouveau windows, flourishing arabesque tower, and lavish interior decorated with wood carvings and azulejos, it was truly palatial. This monument to an affluent past still stands on the seafront promenade amidst a sea of concrete. It no longer carries the same cachet, but it has been renovated and is a quiet and comfortable place to stay (*14 rooms; Avenida Tomás Cabreira; Tel: 240 55 Fax: 415 369; Category 1*)

Although the 'Biarritz' of Portugal has suffered at the hands of the developers, the beach nevertheless remains one of the loveliest coastal stretches in the Algarve. It is so long and wide, you will never have difficulty finding a place to lay down your towel. The sand is fine and soft underfoot, and it is scattered with some impressive rock formations. A good place to go for a sundowner is the *Casa de Chá*, the restaurant in the 17th century fort of *Santa Catarina* that stands over the harbour. ◁▷ There is a fine view from the balcony across the Arade estuary and over to the São João fort on the opposite bank.

Praia da Rocha has ample accommodation, and the local tourist office will willingly supply details of hotels, pensions and apartments. The most exclusive hotel here is the *Hotel Algarve*. It stands on top of the cliffs, has a perfect sea view and a big swimming pool (*220 rooms; Avenida Tomás Cabreira; Tel: 415 001, Fax: 415 999; Category L-1*). Watersports enthusiasts will find plenty to keep them occupied: fishing, water-skiing, sailing and diving facilities are all offered. The *Penina Hotel*, 5 km west of here, has a good golf course as well as tennis and riding facilities.

SAGRES/CABO DE SÃO VICENTE

(A6) ☙ The Algarve's most spectacular stretch of coast runs from Odeceixe down to Cabo de São Vicente. The sea here is too rough for bathing and consequently the area remains relatively unspoilt by tourism. Big breakers roll relentlessly on to the sands, but don't be tempted to brave them; they are deceptively strong. Even paddling can be hazardous, as there are many sharp coral reefs hidden beneath the frothy surf.

The impregnable limestone cliff wall of the cape stands 60 m above the sea and marks the westernmost point of the Algarve and, indeed, Europe. The cape is constantly buffeted by strong winds that blow in from the sea, and is often shrouded in fog, even in summer. ★ ☙ The Cabo de São Vicente lighthouse is a sight that shouldn't be missed. It stands on a high craggy precipice, dominating the skyline, and its beam is visible from a distance of 100 km. The view from the tower (73 steps) is spectacular. The polished prisms within are 150 years old and the light is generated from 3000 watt bulbs. In the eventuality of a power cut, an old petrol burner is always kept ready as a stand in. It is a bracing, desolate place that over the centuries has inspired many tales and legends. It was considered by the Celts to be sacred ground, and was a *promontorium sanctum* for the Greeks and Romans, where the gods came to sleep, and in the Middle Ages it was the Christian site of the 'temple of the Holy Crows' (see page 15). Street traders are out here in all weathers selling, amongst other things, warm woollen jumpers to tourists caught unawares by the bracing winds, or perhaps chilled by the macabre tales.

SIGHTSEEING

Fortaleza do Beliche

☙ Half way between the Cape and Sagres stand the massive boundary walls that enclose the *Fortaleza do Beliche (Tel: 64124)* that stands over a sheltered bay, where ships often anchor for a quiet night. The restaurant is nothing to write home about, but with luck you might be able to get one of the four rooms in the castle. The view from here across the wild and wind-swept landscape is especially stunning at night when the sea is bathed in moonlight. From the small chapel on the edge of the cliff you can watch the seagulls floating on the warm evening air currents that rise from the waters below. An unforgettable sight.

Fortaleza do Infante

☙ The Cabo de São Vicente – Cape Saint Vincent – is 6 km from Sagres and the path that leads to it passes through some dramatic scenery. On a high plateau that faces the Atlantic, this historic spit of land so exposed to the elements is barren and dry. It was almost certainly the site of Henry the Navigator's sailing school and observatory. From this promontory his students would watch their brave colleagues as they set off across the high seas in search of new worlds. A museum is being built here, and unfortunately the youth hostel has had to be closed. The chapel of *Nossa Senhora da Graça* stands here and next to it an impressive stone compass rose.

When the sea rumbles against the rocks below, the locals say that 'the giant is breathing'. Over thousands of years the cliffs have been eroded by the waves that bubble and spray through the gaping holes and crevices that have been carved out by them. If you can afford to, a lovely place to stay is the *Pousada do Infante (39 rooms); Tel: 64222/23, Fax 64225; Category 1)* a lovely mansion on the cliffs just before the fishing district of Sagres.

There are three lovely beaches in this area worth a mention: the beach in front of the *Baleeira Hotel* is particularly renowned for its naturally formed rock lobster traps; while behind the hotel are the quieter and more isolated beaches of *Martinhal* and *Robolinhos* .

RESTAURANT

A Tasca

❂ Nowhere else in the Algarve is the choice of fish and seafood as wide as it is in Sagres. Swordfish, sharks, sea eels, giant perch, as well as crabs, lobster, and squid are all fished endlessly from its waters – all of which appear on the menu of this popular rustic restaurant. It is situated directly above the harbour and has a lovely balcony to eat on.
Daily (except Sat); Category 2

HOTELS

Hotel da Baleeira

Central and practical, it stands by a lovely beach.
120 rooms; Sagres; Tel: 64212/13; Category 2

Motel Gambozinos

This attractive hotel, approximately 3 km from Sagres, stands on a fine sandy bay. Just 500 m into the bay lie the Martinhal Islands, a nature reserve which provide the nesting ground for hundreds of different species of birds. The restaurant near the bird sanctuary is somewhat over-priced, but has a nice bar on the beach, which is ideal for children.
17 rooms; Praia do Martinhal/Sagres; Tel: 64318; Category 2

SPORT & LEISURE

Sagres is an angler's paradise, especially for those who like to fish from boats. For further information on boats for hire, just ask at the *tasca*, or in the tourist office. Wind surfing and diving facilities are also available.

INFORMATION

Posto de Turismo

Daily 09.00-19.00 hrs; Fortaleza de Sagres; Tel: 64125

The home of friendship

The Portuguese have a reputation for their warmth and hospitality. As the Spanish say, 'If friendship had a home, then it would be Portugal'

Practical information

*Important addresses and information for your
visit to the Algarve*

BANKS

Opening hours are Mon-Fri
08.30-15.00 hrs. The bank at Faro
airport, however, stays open all
day until 19.30 hrs, although it
shuts for lunch around midday.

BUSES & COACHES

Portugal's bus network is widespread and relatively efficient.
The state-run company is the
Rodoviária Nacional and the central bus station is in Faro (*behind the
Hotel Eva, Avenida da República*).
They have a fleet of coaches
called *Rápidos* running between
all the larger towns and most of
the remote inland communities
are well served. The privately run
luxury coaches, or *Espressos,* are
equipped with air-conditioning
and television, and reach Lisbon
in just four hours. *Ports of call: Lagos, Rossio São João; Portimão, Largo
Dique 2-4.*

CAMPING

Camping on unauthorized sites is
illegal. Information on camp-sites
is available from the *Federação
Portuguesa de Campismo, Rua da*
*Voz do Operário 1, 1000 Lisboa; Tel:
01/ 886 2350.* The camp-sites in
Albufeira and *Olhão* are particularly nice.

CAR HIRE

Car rental in Portugal is relatively cheap and, although the
roads can be rough, it is a good
way to get around. Bear in mind,
however, that the Portuguese do
have a reputation for reckless
driving, so you will need to be
vigilant. The speed limit on
motorways is 120 kph, 90 kph on
other roads and 60 kph in built
up areas. You must be over 21 to
hire a car and wearing a seat belt
is compulsory. Petrol prices are
roughly as follows: 1 litre of 4-
star (*super* – don't bother with the
normal) costs about 155$00. Un-
leaded petrol (*sem chumbo*) costs
between 152 and 155$00, and
these days it is available from
most petrol stations. In case of an
accident you should always call
the police, although they will
probably take a while to arrive on
the scene.

Most car rental agencies oper-
ating in the Algarve have an office

at Faro airport, but it usually works out cheaper to pre-arrange car hire. If you do decide to rent on the spot, it's worth shopping around first as prices can vary substantially.

You can hire mopeds from about £6 per day including insurance. Try *Moto Sonho; Rua Dr Joaquim Telo 27, 8600 Lagos; Tel: 082/767 571.*

CAMPER VANS

Camper vans can be hired in Lisbon. A Pilote 390 which accommodates 2-4 people, for example, costs between £100 and £130 per day, while a Ford Delta for 5 people costs between £70 and £110, including transfer from the airport, insurance and unlimited mileage.

CHEMISTS

There are *farmácias* in almost every village and town in Portugal. A wide range of drugs are available without prescription and medication is relatively cheap. Pharmacists are qualified for consultation on minor ailments. A list of chemists on late-night and weekend duty is usually printed in the local paper, or you can ask at the tourist office.

CHILDREN

Portugal is a very child friendly country and young families are always welcome in hotels and restaurants. If you need a baby-sitter, enquire at your hotel reception or at the local tourist office and they should be able to provide you with the name and address of a reliable child-minder.

CUSTOMS

Although customs restrictions have now been lifted for goods imported between EU countries (provided they are for personal use), there are, nevertheless, certain recommended restrictions: 90 l wine, 10 l spirits, 20 l fortified wine, 200 cigars and 800 cigarettes.

DOCTORS

If you need an English-speaking doctor, the British or American consul (see below for phone numbers) should be able to supply you with the address of one in your area. Alternatively ask at your hotel or at the tourist office. The larger hospitals are in Faro and Portimão, but every town has its own health centre (*Centro da Saúde*). The *Casa de Saúde Santa Maria de Faro (Tel 089/802106)* is a good private hospital and the staff and doctors speak English.

ELECTRICITY

A wattage of 220 Volts applies in Portugal. For UK appliances, a continental adaptor can be obtained from most travel accessory outlets, and some airport shops also stock them.

EMBASSIES & CONSULATES

Portuguese consulates
in Britain:
62 Brompton Road, London SW3 1BJ; Tel: 0171-581 8722

in Ireland:
Knockshinna House, Knockshinna St., Fox Rock, Dublin 18; Tel: 01-289 4416

in the USA:
2125 Kalorama Rd NY; Washington DC 2008; Tel: 202- 328 8610

Consulates/Embassies in Lisbon

British consulate:
Rua São Domingos à Lapa 37; Tel: 396 11 91

Irish embassy:
Rua da Imprensa à Estrêla 1 (4th floor); Tel: 396 15 69

US embassy:
Avenida das Forças Armadas; Tel: 726 66 00

EMERGENCY NUMBERS

Police, fire and ambulance: 115
Faro hospital: 089/803427
Emergency veterinary surgeon: 089/415786

HIKING

The best time of year to explore the countryside of the Algarve is either in spring or autumn; the summer months are not ideal for hiking as it gets too hot. There are some wonderful nature trails, both along the coast and inland, and most tourist offices will provide maps of local scenic routes on request.

NEWSPAPERS

Newsagents, bookshops and kiosks in Faro, Portimão, and the large holiday resorts stock a wide range of international publications. You can find most of the English national dailies here, as well as the *International Herald Tribune*, although they appear on the shelves one day late. The *Algarve Magazine* and *Discover the Algarve* are local publications written in English and aimed at tourists. Both magazines are distributed in the main tourist areas.

POLICE

The branch of the police force you would be most likely to have to deal with are the PSP − the *Polícia de Segurança de Pública.* Dressed in grey uniforms bearing the local coat of arms, they are hard to miss. One of their primary functions is traffic control, and they can be pretty ruthless when it comes to giving parking tickets. The rural police wear a green band around their hats, and can often be seen patrolling on horseback. They are part of the *Guarda Nacional Republicana* (GNR). The police officers you see patrolling the main roads and motorways in their white cars and big motorbikes are known as the *Brigada de Trânsito*. They also control traffic and can be tough on anyone they catch breaking the rules of the road. Radar speed checks are fairly common, and anyone caught speeding is immediately submitted to a breathalyser test.

PORTUGUESE

Portuguese is a Romance language. When written you can see the similarities with other Latin languages, but when spoken it sounds more Slavonic than Southern European. Characterized by its soft and nasal sounds (ão, ãe), it is softer than Spanish and has a melodic ring to it. Words are mostly stressed on the penultimate syllable. Exceptions are marked by acute accents over the vowels which show where the stress should fall. The language is spoken very quickly which makes comprehension difficult. This very basic list of words may come in handy:

hello (good morning): *bom día*
hello (good afternoon): *boa tarde*
good night: *boa noite*
Goodbye: *até a vista, adeus*
please: *por favor*
thank you: *obrigado* (if you are a man); *obrigada* (if you are a woman)
sorry: *desculpe*
how much is it?: *quanto custa?*
Could I have the bill please: *faz favor, a conta*

POST & TELEPHONE

Post offices are indicated by the sign *Correio* or CTT. Opening times are Mon-Fri 08.30-12.30 and 14.30-18.00 hrs. The main post offices and the branch at the airport are also open on Saturdays until midday, while the main post offices in Lisbon have extended opening hours. A letter sent within Europe takes on average five days to reach its destination, and letters to America can take up to 10 days to get there. If you want your mail to arrive more speedily you should use the *Correio Azul* express service. Stamps (*selos*) can be bought not only from post offices but also from many shops and hotels, and anywhere you see a red horse – the national post and communications symbol. Letters and postcards within Europe cost 78$00 and 130$00 outside Europe.

Most post offices now have fax machines, but the service is expensive, as are telegrams.

International telephone calls can be made from main post offices, or from telephone kiosks marked *internacionais*. Phone cards make telephoning abroad easier, as you don't have to worry about feeding the box with coins as you speak. Known as *Credifon* cards, they cost from 750$00 and can be bought from post offices and some newspaper kiosks.

To place an international call first dial 00, then the country code (UK 44; Ireland 353; USA 1) followed by the area code omitting the first 0, and lastly the subscriber number. To phone Portugal from abroad you need to dial the international access code followed by the code for Portugal (351), then the area code (without the 0) followed by the number.

Local calls: The Algarve has three different dialling codes: Sagres to Albufeira; 082, Albufeira to Fuzeta; 089, and Fuzeta to Vila Real de Santo António; 081. For Lisbon dial 01 and for directory enquiries 118.

TOURIST INFORMATION

Região de Turismo do Algarve
Avenida 5 de Outubro, 8000 Faro; Tel 089/800 400

Portuguese Tourist and Information office
In the UK:
22, Sackville Street, London W1; Tel: 0171- 494 1441

in Ireland:
Enquire at the Irish embassy for tourist information (see page 91)

in the USA:
590 Fifth Avenue, 4th floor, New York 10036; Tel: 212-354 4403

ESSENTIALS

YOUTH HOSTELS

The south of Portugal has the most youth hostels in the country. The oldest of these is in the castle in Sagres, but unfortunately it is closed for renovation. The youth hostel in Portimão is comfortable and well-equipped with a swimming pool set in a garden, and a billiard room (*Lugar do Cocam, Maravilhosas, Portimão; Tel: 082/ 85704*). The hostel in Lagos offers the same comfort, but has no pool (*Rua Lançarote de Freitas 50; Tel: 082/761 970*). The hostel in Faro is small and basic (*Rua da P.S.P.; Tel 089/801970*).

For further information:
Associação Portuguesa de Pousadas da Juventude, Rua Andrade Corvo 46, 1000, Lisboa; Tel: 01/442 6185
YHA England and Wales: Tel: 0171-836 1036
YHA Ireland: Tel: 01-830 4555
YHA USA: 202-783 6161

WEATHER IN FARO
Seasonal averages

Day-time temperatures in °C

Jan	Feb	Mar	Apr	May	June	July	Aug	Sep	Oct	Nov	Dec
15	16	18	20	22	25	28	28	26	22	19	16

Night-time temperatures in °C

Jan	Feb	Mar	Apr	May	June	July	Aug	Sep	Oct	Nov	Dec
9	10	11	13	14	18	20	20	19	16	13	10

Sunshine: hours per day

Jan	Feb	Mar	Apr	May	June	July	Aug	Sep	Oct	Nov	Dec
6	7	7	9	10	12	12	12	10	8	6	6

Rainfall: days per month

Jan	Feb	Mar	Apr	May	June	July	Aug	Sep	Oct	Nov	Dec
7	6	8	5	3	1	0	0	2	4	7	7

Sea temperatures in °C

Jan	Feb	Mar	Apr	May	June	July	Aug	Sep	Oct	Nov	Dec
15	15	15	16	17	18	19	20	20	19	17	16

Do's and don'ts

How to avoid some of the traps and pitfalls the unwary traveller may face

Rubbish
The Portuguese authorities are still grappling with the problem of clearing the piles of refuse which accumulate in the streets. Rubbish bins, however, are plentiful and are emptied twice weekly. Glass is recycled and you'll find bottle banks in all the major resort areas.

Sewage
Although it is prohibited in Portugal there are still some places where sewage is dumped directly into the sea. It's best to closely inspect the beach on which you're planning to swim. Sewage and refuse are also disposed of in the River Arcade by Portimão. A boat trip rather than a swim would be more advisable on this pretty river.

Chemicals in the Guadiana
You would be ill-advised to go swimming in this border river, as Spain still dumps chemical waste into its tributaries.

The slowness of officials
You'll probably find the service in post-offices and banks to be frustratingly slow. Complaining, however, will get you nowhere.

The only thing to do is adopt the Latin attitude: *tenha paciência* – be patient – a piece of advice the Portuguese are fond of giving.

Shellfish
Shellfish have become quite expensive in Portugal. In order to avoid an unpleasant surprise when your bill comes, it's best to ascertain prices beforehand (menu prices are usually given per kilo).

Protecting the coastline
Although you may see many Portuguese taking their cars on to the dunes, eg at Praia do Ancão, it is something you should avoid doing as it destroys the flora and fauna.

Quarteira
This resort, like so many that have sprung up along the coast, has sadly lost its original charm. The main road running along the beach is lined with huge concrete blocks several rows deep. Armação is much the same. Its only advantage is that the beach extends for miles in both directions. If you venture out, however, you can find quieter stretches of beach, away from the built up area.

INDEX

This index lists all the places mentioned in this guide. Page numbers in bold indicate the main entry in the case of multiple references, italics indicate photos

What do you get for your money?

The national currency is the escudo, represented by a dollar sign written in the middle of the price. Notes come in denominations of 500, 1000, 2000, 5000, and 10 000 escudos and there are coins of 1, 2.50, 5, 10, 15, 20, 50, 100 and 200 escudos. The current exchange rate is around 230$00 to the pound (October 1996). You should bring about 5000$00 with you, but it's best to change the rest of your money in Portugal, – local rates are more favourable. The big banks will give you the best deals. Eurocheques are accepted in most hotels and shops. The maximum amount you can issue a Eurocheque for is 35,000$00 (*trinta e cinco mil escudos*); they are accepted in most hotels and many retail outlets. The major credit cards (Visa, Mastercard, American Express, Eurocard) are also widely accepted by hotels, restaurants and shops. You can also use them to withdraw cash from the automatic cash dispensers found in most big towns.

Typical prices: you can get a decent bottle of wine for around £2; concert and theatre tickets can cost from £6 to £11; entrance into museums is 100$00-250$00; a good meal in a country restaurant shouldn't cost more than £7 including wine.

£	Esc	Esc	£
1.00	230	250	1.09
2.00	460	500	2.17
3.00	690	750	3.26
4.00	920	1000	4.35
5.00	1 150	1500	6.52
7.50	1 725	2000	8.70
10.00	2 300	3000	13.00
12.50	2 875	4000	17.40
15.00	3 450	5000	21.75
20.00	4 600	6000	26.00
25.00	5 750	7500	32.60
30.00	6 900	10 000	43.50
35.00	8 050	15 000	65.20
40.00	9 200	20 000	87.00
50.00	11 500	30 000	130.00
75.00	17 250	40 000	174.00
100.00	23 000	50 000	217.00
250.00	57 500	75 000	326.00
500.00	115 000	100 000	435.00

MARCO POLO
SPANISH

Speaking made easy

with
Local Tips

How to get more from your holiday!

Use Marco Polo Language Guides to understand, and be understood.

- Phrases for every situation
- Do's and don'ts
- Complete menus
- Travelling with kids
- Over 1 000 of the most important words you're ever likely to need – and Local Tips!

These language guides are for you!

How do I say it? – made easy!